Afrosonic Life

Afrosonic Life

Mark V. Campbell

BLOOMSBURY ACADEMIC
NEW YORK • LONDON • OXFORD • NEW DELHI • SYDNEY

BLOOMSBURY ACADEMIC
Bloomsbury Publishing Inc
1385 Broadway, New York, NY 10018, USA
50 Bedford Square, London, WC1B 3DP, UK
29 Earlsfort Terrace, Dublin 2, Ireland

BLOOMSBURY, BLOOMSBURY ACADEMIC and the Diana logo
are trademarks of Bloomsbury Publishing Plc

First published in the United States of America 2022
This paperback edition published 2023

Copyright © Mark V. Campbell, 2022

For legal purposes the Acknowledgments on p. viii constitute
an extension of this copyright page.

Cover design by Louise Dugdale
Cover image: 'OG Boombox' by Leon 'Eklipz' Robinson

All rights reserved. No part of this publication may be reproduced or transmitted in any form or by any means, electronic or mechanical, including photocopying, recording, or any information storage or retrieval system, without prior permission in writing from the publishers.

Bloomsbury Publishing Inc does not have any control over, or responsibility for, any third-party websites referred to or in this book. All internet addresses given in this book were correct at the time of going to press. The author and publisher regret any inconvenience caused if addresses have changed or sites have ceased to exist, but can accept no responsibility for any such changes.

Library of Congress Cataloging-in-Publication Data
Names: Campbell, Mark V., author.
Title: Afrosonic life / Mark V. Campbell.
Description: New York : Bloomsbury Academic, 2022. | Includes bibliographical references and index. | Summary: "Explores the role sonic innovations in the African diaspora play in articulating methodologies for living the afterlife of slavery"– Provided by publisher.
Identifiers: LCCN 2021040174 (print) | LCCN 2021040175 (ebook) |
ISBN 9781501379291 (hardback) | ISBN 9781501379338 (paperback) |
ISBN 9781501379307 (epub) | ISBN 9781501379314 (pdf) |
ISBN 9781501379321 (ebook other)
Subjects: LCSH: Popular music–African influences. | Blacks–Music–History and criticism. | Turntablism. | Remixes–History and criticism.
Classification: LCC ML3470.C366 2022 (print) | LCC ML3470 (ebook) | DDC 781.64–dc23
LC record available at https://lccn.loc.gov/2021040174
LC ebook record available at https://lccn.loc.gov/2021040175

ISBN:	HB:	978-1-5013-7929-1
	PB:	978-1-5013-7933-8
	ePDF:	978-1-5013-7931-4
	eBook:	978-1-5013-7930-7

Typeset by Integra Software Services Pvt. Ltd.

To find out more about our authors and books visit www.bloomsbury.com
and sign up for our newsletters.

For my Suns, stay shining

Contents

Acknowledgments	viii
Introduction	1
1 Soundman/Sound System (S.W. rmx)	13
2 Turning the Tables	43
3 Riddim Science: On Living Hip-Hop's Sonic Innovations	67
4 Dubbing the Remix and Its Uses	91
Conclusion: Come Rewind/We Were the 1st Robots	119
Bibliography	124
Index	135

Acknowledgments

The village that made this possible is vast and any absences in the forthcoming list is simply an indication of my own failings. I have been blessed to have the following in my life, encouraging, supporting and supporting some more. First of all to the whole unit, Gena, Kai and Xavier; Pops, Miss Eddie and Dawny; DJ Pyscho Soul & Capt'n; the Triple 'S' mans dem Jake D'Snake, Grimlock, Bonez, UA; The Bigger than Hip-Hop family (R.I.P. Rofromtheboro); the entire team at Northside Hip-Hop. DTS, Kolor Brown, Eklipz & Jwyze bless up for holding me down. Centre Table peeps, good lookin out.

There are so many artists and scholars that have been generous in their ideas and time. Thank you nourbeSe philip, Katherine McKittrick, Rinaldo Walcott, Alissa Trotz, Sylvia Wynter, Alexander Weheliye, Murray Forman, Barrington Walker, Pablo Idahosa, Lina Sunseri, Joy Mannette, Carl E. James, Andrea Davis, Leslie Sanders, Kristin Moriah, Davina Bhadahar, Kathleen Pirrie-Adams, Camille Hernandez-Ramdwar, Lyndon Philip, Simone Browne, Andrea Fatona, OmiSoore Dryden, Kulsoom Anwer Shaikh, Sam Tecle, Muna Dahir, Felicia Mings, Pamela Edmonds, Michele Pearson Clarke, Kevin Ormsby, Michael Chambers, Michie Mee, Killowatt Soundcrew, Barry Boothe of TKO Sound, Nadia Bello, Dionne Brand (for the shoes bonding moments), and Robin Elliot and Laura Risk for your feedback on earlier drafts of this work. Ajay Heble, Charity Marsh for early investments in me, Barry Freeman, Maydianne Andrande, Lynn Tucker and Roger Mantie for making UTSC home.

The patience, generosity and skillful eyes of the team at Bloomsbury have been indispensible to the making of this publication. Thank you Leah Babb-Rosenfeld, Rachel Moore, Rebecca Willford, and the reviewers for pointing me in the right direction.

I cannot forget the vast and multiple supporters, Social Science & Humanities Research Council, The Jackman Humanities Centre, the Black Research Network, the Connaught New Scholar award and the team at the Black Studies Summer Seminar.

Introduction

When learning to DJ as a teenager, me and my crew, Triple 'S', would bring together our set, two turntables, a mixer and an amplifier at one of our parent's basements. We were learning how to manipulate vinyl records and replicate the skills we heard DJs demonstrate on the radio and on mixtapes. One member of my crew, the mathematician, known as 'Exmadecimals', developed a theory that called for a manual rewinding of a vinyl record counter-clockwise seven times to bring the record back to its beginning – he called it the Law of Seven. This was one of the skills highly celebrated in hip-hop culture we sought to develop: to quickly bring records back to the beginning to repeat the opening bars of the track. At the time, in the early 1990s, I hadn't learned how to count bars, hadn't heard of the 12-bar blues and had no concern for any other elements of a song beyond its kick drum and bass line. A successful bringing back of the first beat of the record meant rotating counter-clockwise through seven revolutions of the vinyl with the crossfader closed (so that the rewinding sound remained in the DJ's headphones only) within the same time frame as the first eight bars of the song playing in real time. This skill demonstrated one's dexterity, timing and rhythm – this sense of physicality was more valued in hip-hop DJ circles and firmly established one as part of the legacy of hip-hop as opposed to house, reggae or techno DJs, who were uniformly less hands on. Unlike today's DJs, we had no digital interface which meant we had to develop a tactile relationship with the first groove on each record; our fingertips had to learn to feel the kick drum or bass line before we could successfully bring the beat back and repeat the opening bars of a track. The Law of Seven had to be combined with a kinaesthetic practice of touching the vinyl and feeling the track's first downbeat.

I never developed another theory of DJing as a teenager, nor did anyone else in my DJ crew. Instead, I laboured to practice the Law of Seven whenever possible. The skill of bringing the beat back required a mathematical understanding of the song structure, a tactile relationship with the grooves implanted on a vinyl record and the counter-clockwise revolutions needed to produce the form of repetition deemed aesthetically pleasing – at least to DJs and their audiences. The Law of Seven connected a cultural aesthetic preference with mathematical reasoning and a kinaesthetic method to reverse the progress of the track. In demonstrating this skill, we DJs lengthened the song, extended the listening or dancing pleasure of our audiences and refused the manufacturer's logic of this vinyl recording and common notions of linearity. These vinyl recordings – promotional tools for the record industry and retail consumer items – became, in the hands of DJs, something more akin to raw musical matter destined to contribute to sonic landscapes yet to be imagined.

This book is that imagining. In developing a DJ practice, techniques like the counter-clockwise reversals of the vinyl record became methods, a praxis for living within, and opaquely beyond, the desires of industry, capital, linear time and Eurocentric musical logic. Nestled somewhere between entertainer and artist, the figure of the DJ (and their decades spent experimenting with vinyl records and audiences) has become my window into the myriad ways in which Black life invents Afrosonic practices, relationalities and logics. The creative labour time of DJing, combined with an irreverence for linear time and an investment in (re)producing oral and aural Afrodiasporic aesthetics produced, for me, contemporary Afrosonic life as a B-side to Western modernity – a relational experience.[1] Throughout this book, I spend time with various music technologies, both analogue and digital, fully cognizant of the generations of Senegambian Griots whose memory work, songs and musical existence pre-date the post-Middle Passage period in focus in this project.

To invoke the notion of a B-side locates this work in a mode that remembers and appreciates our digital present's analogue ancestry. While both audio cassettes and vinyl records had B-sides to their physical mediums, my immediate concern here is with recorded vinyl. To think about the record and its relevancy to A-side and B-side playing modes involves understanding the role of the turntable in making one side of a record audible, while relegating the other side of the

---

[1] After DJing radio shows featuring all B-sides and remixes during the days of vinyl, this notion of a B-side to modernity I found in an essay by Rinaldo Walcott, 'Salted Cod: Black Canadian and Diasporic Sensibilities' published in 2006 as a catalogue essay to Andrea Fatona's Canada-wide exhibition, *Reading the Image: Poetics of the Black Diaspora*. Needless to say, this idea has resonated with me ever since.

medium to silence, despite both sides being intimately conjoined as one record. Often, there exists a relationship between the songs on each side of a record, with James Brown often placing part 2 of his songs on the B-side and producers such as King Tubby also creating other versions of the A-side or another song on the B-side. Clearly, one can discern the physical relationship between both sides of a vinyl record, while the sonic relationship is not always immediately perceivable. The work of the DJ in handling and manipulating each side of a record invents new relations unrelated to the physical medium, yet in conversation with the sound encoded onto the vinyl and various technologies since the invention of the phonograph. With the turntable central to my analysis, I am attentive to its 'misuse' as a musical instrument and centre notions of recursive time as a disruption of Western linear time. My refusal to simply forget the potency of the B-side (and its plethora of potent remixes) long after manufacturers have made the concept void, is a sort of recursive logic that emanates directly from the various sonic innovations in focus here.[2]

More specifically, by exploring what myriad Afrosonic musical innovations do, this work zeroes in on the musical and sonic practices of Black life. Black musical forms in the diaspora find interesting ways to invent themselves within colonial regimes, outside of market logic and aligned with a respect for Black creative forms that mitigate dehumanization. These forms of musical and sonic innovations are intriguing starting points to consider and reconsider Black life in the diaspora. Afrosonic life is the wading through, the wandering with, and the enjoyment of the multiple ways Black people make music with an affective impact that cannot be contained by the entertainment industry. In the following pages, I explore, with hesitation – for I know that sound quickly overwhelms the written word – a question that has fuelled my thinking for the last two decades: how are we still here, and what role does music play in our sustenance?

Even in attempting to arrive at a half decent answer to this question, which perhaps should be reserved for the elders, the multitude of possibilities overflow the page and prove my initial question's inadequacy. Instead of trying to answer this question, this book wanders through and connects the faintly

---

[2] Thank you nourbeSe for reading the earliest version of my ideas and pointing me towards the oriki praise singers. In both the Yoruban and Ghanaian contexts, I have found much alignment with the oriki defined by Barber as 'attributions or appellations ... addressed to a subject'. This early lead was a reminder this project was on the right track. For an in-depth ethnographic study, see Barber (2020).

related in an attempt to piece together a narrative of being human long hidden by opaque creative inventions, for instance dub music or capoeira. These creative inventions and art forms have proven over the centuries and decades to be a site in which Black life flourishes often mitigating undesirable social realities. Further, following cues from scholars Aaron Kamugisha, Clinton Hutton, Rinaldo Walcott, Alexander Weheliye, Sylvia Wynter and Katherine McKittrick, I read these sites of creative activity as rich arenas to posit otherworldly possibilities for Black living. My desire to explore possibilities for Black musical life in conversation with scholars outside of the study of music is a gesture to the necessary relationality in scholarly work needed to attend to the possibilities of liberation at the core of Black studies.

Many of the ideas shared in this book are made possible by taking seriously Black joy and the sonic architecture that make possible the numerous musical innovations across the African diaspora. My insistence in centring Black joy in my work is both a pedagogical and a methodological choice.[3] Black musical expressions induce moments of joy, and these moments tell us about the constricting practices of expressions of dominant notions of comportment and expressiveness. Black joy, in its momentary episodes and bursts, also reveals the fragility of the social organization of Western post-Middle Passage culture in which legal dehumanization was to orchestrate a system of ensuring objecthood and labour. Methodologically, the affective responses of Black life enjoying music, the shouts, the stomps, the furnace pounding[4] and the soul claps reveal the importance of a multisensory expression and experience of Black music. Inspired by the music scholarship of Guthrie Ramsey, Mark Butler, Dylan Robinson, Ellie Hisama, Michael Veal and Samuel Floyd (amongst others), this project is invested in a praxis that embraces a decolonizing of music studies, a centring of affect and an insistence on relationality. My positionality has an interiority to it as a DJ whose responsibility has been to keep people dancing and to induce emphatic enunciations of joy. Neither the eyes nor the ears alone suffice when listening, co-creating and responding to the experiential stimuli the DJ harnesses with two turntables. Attentiveness to the joy music brings to Black life necessarily means this project divests from the circulation of Black

---

[3] My focus on pleasure and joy is not meant to obscure the sacred and ceremonial rituals also connected to various Black musics, such as the traditions within Candomblé and music of the Abakuá.

[4] I include this practice of furnace slapping with Christopher Small's 'musicking' to inject a specific Afrodiasporic practice in Canada in which basement parties in the winter become home to this emotive practice and response.

pain – a focus that obscures the multiple ways Afrodiasporic populations have invented forms of living in conditions not of their making.

For more than half a century, Jamaican sound system culture (including Columbian Picós, UK and various other globally situated sound systems) have consistently been a source of joy, innovation and life. Jamaican sound systems form the backbone of this book because they amaze me. They have mastered techniques of bringing happiness to masses of Black people. Another part of the reason why sound systems amaze me is because they represent a counter-world of values, largely unbothered by the dominant culture. They are, as Julian Henriques details in *Sonic Bodies*, steeped in a relationality that is hard to disconnect from the joy they bring. Through their multisensory efforts, connecting our aural, kinaesthetic and oral realities, sound systems create moments when Afrodiasporic life flourishes, unfettered by the weight of racializing schemas invested in a fabricated hierarchical ordering of our world. In this book, I argue that Afrosonic innovations provide methods and metaphors for Black life beyond the racial logics advanced by European colonialization and continually reasserted by logics of white supremacy. Sonic innovations are creative texts that, as McKittrick astutely notes, 'create conditions through which relationality, rebellion, conversation, interdisciplinarity, and disobedience are fostered' (2021: 51). As such, they are the building blocks, the soft infrastructure, upon which subjectivities defy and disregard the ocular-centric logic of Western European's version of the human as 'Man'.

The Afrosonic innovations examined here are disinterested in the effectiveness of legal and liberalist notions of 'freedom', much to the dismay of various scholars interested in slavery and emancipation. Instead, these innovations gesture towards and articulate a notion of liberation that lies outside or beyond the liberal humanist language of British, Dutch, Spanish and French colonizers. Spirituals, such as 'Follow the Drinking Gourd', are instructive here, facilitating a notion of self that binds one's racialized reality with a subjectivity embedded in sound. The encoded instructions to assist runaways in acts of self-liberation via sound are cognizant of the racial ordering that makes one's enslavement possible. The spiritual formulates itself around the existence of a racial schema, adding a lyrical map to freedom, a tool not reliant on the laws and letters of the land. For those in the fields singing 'Swing Low, Sweet Chariot', sending these encoded messages to runaways was about subscribing to a sonic subjectivity as a subversive method to liberation. Yet, even singing spirituals were not without controversy, as improvised and publicly sung spirituals became a problem in the public sphere in 1819 in Philadelphia, with complaints registered by white church members (Southern 1997: 180).

Those who used song to orally detail pathways to north of the Mason-Dixie Line were immersed in a performative agency that sought to transform the relations of power, on an individual level, and to mitigate the impacts of racial violence. To simply take part in oral maps to 'freedom' is to quintessentially participate in a definition of freedom relayed through sound – a contingent liberation that is not necessarily aligned with capital accumulation or the free market. While 'Negro Spirituals' later entered the market, yielding donations and eventually record sales, this was not their original intent. These songs, like many of the creative outputs of Afrodiasporic life were commoditized. But in their original form in the fields, spirituals had no market orientation and thus evaded a semantic trap of liberal humanism propagated by those invested in the transformation of the formerly enslaved into an emergent consumer class.

Sonic innovations unravel the 'rules' that govern our present social hierarchy proposing a ground upon which Afrodiasporic people's expressions of human life that might diverge from reproducing a conception of the human focused on phenotypes (Wynter 1992: 271). The subversion of technologies, from mixing boards to turntables, produces rehumanizing sonic subjectivities that form the core of understanding sonic innovations as presenting a new language from which to reshape social reality.

Method

In this work, I embrace Alexander Weheliye's notion of sound thinking. Methodologically, I work through various sounds, songs and sonic formations generously interpreting what living and creating in the 'red' might offer, riffing both Tricia Rose's use of the term in *Black Noise* and Jaylib's 2004 track 'The Red'. I embrace the unauthorized remixes and the sounds and practices in which the field of musicology finds little value, placing significant emphasis on sound systems, DJs and the mixtape, in all of its illegal entanglements, regardless of disciplinary interests in the study of music. Weheliye's 'thinking sound/sound thinking' allows this project to attune itself to the role of technology in sonic innovations. He offers us a theory of the phonograph that 'blends sensation and perception and listens to their variety and intensity in their co-mingling' (2005: 36). In working with Weheliye's concept of phonographies, I centre multisensory engagements with Black music and remain attentive to multiple modes of relationality that structure the creation, expression and reception of sonic innovations. Such attentiveness is also focused on the role of technology in making possible mixes, remixes, dubs, rhymes and turntablism. The desire to witness the commingling of oral, aural, kinaesthetic and technological experiences structure the lens by which relational modes embedded in Afrosonic innovations are uncovered. This work and its desires are powered by a Black studies framework explicitly invested in tools and tactics that might make Black liberation possible. Following the kinds of liberatory frameworks Katherine McKittrick offers in *Dear Science and Other Stories*, this project – already invested in the 'rehumanizing' potentials of Black musical formations – is interested in multiple and intersecting disciplinary approaches to analyzing Afrosonic innovations.

The works explored in this project do not neatly fall into the category of popular music, nor are they of concern to those in the cultural industries. Instead, the sonic innovations explored here offer methods for inventing Black life in ways that diverge from common place or normalized ways of musical experience. By operating in the 'red' and appreciating transgressive demonic grounds, musical genre also does not neatly tie together this project, as I move between reggae, hip-hop, turntablism electro mash-ups and unauthorized remixes.

My investment in the term sonic is a deliberate move to inclusively work with a variety of sounds and sound-making practices that are not limited to music, particularly in its commodified form. In an attempt to widen my analysis beyond market-orientated and exchange-value music, the term sonic is deployed here as a way of becoming attentive to sonar frequencies invented to be audible to the human ear. Capturing the attention of the human ear is a central way in which the forced commodification of Africans was interrupted and as a way to demonstrate one's humanity by seeking refuge within the frequencies available to the human ear. By focusing on innovations, the continuous invention of sounds by Afrodiasporic people becomes central to my analysis, moving beyond what is manufactured and focusing on what is invented and emitted within or without industry infrastructure but always in relation to the people, the audiences.

Sounds exist with or without the audibility of human ears, but the sonic is intimately related to the human senses, but not necessarily human intelligibility. The sonic is a more useful relation in this project not just due to the centrality of human audibility but also because the sonic is also a specific relation to the speed of soundwaves. It illuminates how time as speed is connected to what and how we hear. The movement of soundwaves at specific speeds centres relations of time. A sonic boom features sounds at ranges beyond the human ear, reminding us of the co-relation between time and sound necessary for human audibility. This co-relation of sound and time is at the heart of how the sonic operates in this book, furthering this relationship to make movement a necessary coordinate in sonic innovations. Audience participation and the physicality of sound and music making are inseparable aspects of sonic innovations in the African diaspora. Sonic innovations as formulated in this project then are about relations of recursive time, physicality and audiences as stimulated by technologies. These relations reoccur throughout various sonic innovations explored in this book, relations of time frequently occur as rhythmic, repetitions and circular. I work to keep sound as sonic relation always entangled within historical time, real time and recursive/cyclical time. This – at times messy – arrangement makes more complex the ways DJs and sound systems engage music (and more), but also it is a generative way to exercise multisensory interrogations of Black life.

The analysis forwarded here then is about the relation of sound to human audibility, not necessarily intelligibility – about time working in multifaceted ways with and through multiple sensory relations. By using the term sonic innovation, I am activating a relationality that evades constricting forms of knowing, that are not easily captured by market forces and refuse to disentangle the multisensory realities that enhance the effect of sound. The notion of a sonic subjectivity then refers to one's heightened awareness of the ways in which sound is consciously prioritized, impacting one's perceptions, beliefs and actions. It is an understanding of one's social location and positioning as invested in sound in ways that mitigate the ocular metrics and racial schemas of Eurocentric life.

Sonic subjectivities in this work operate as a specific awareness of sound and its relational existence to the visual assemblages of race. I build on Weheliye's sonic Afro-modernity, with 'the subject as an indeterminate sonic opacity', which exists as a texture and a vibe beyond intelligibility, located in a sonorous sensuality pivoting on a multisensory oral, aural and kinaesthetic relationality (2005: 68). For Weheliye, 'a subject of sonic Afro-modernity … comes into being in the crevice made by the audiovisual disjunction engendered by the phonograph' (70). Extending Weheliye beyond the phonograph to include the turntable, mixtape and the mixing board, I posit that sonic subjectivities do not just lie at this disjuncture but also are invented through the active manipulation of music technologies to exit the normative relations of Western music making and logic. Sonic subjectivities become possible in the space between the intended use and the actual misuse of sound technologies, both analogue and digital. Audibility to the human ear is central and the leveraging of technology to achieve another human modality that loosens the grasp of phenotypes and their accompanying hierarchical orderings.

Since sonic life is at the heart of this project, Jamaica and its music, with its many sonic innovations, pervade multiple chapters in this book. For an island of less than three million people, the impact of their musical creations have resonated globally, both before the popularity of Robert Nestor Marley and now in our digital present. Undeniably, diaspora underpins how and when Jamaica's music and sonic innovations spread across the world. From the 1958 Windrush generation in the United Kingdom to the more recent explosion of Jamaican musical talent in Miami, the movement of Jamaicans has brought ska, rocksteady, dub, reggae and dancehall to various metropolitan locations. One could also argue for the diasporic resonance of Trinidad's steelpan as an earlier Caribbean musical innovation. The same could be said about the importance of Samba or rhumba in diaspora and amongst diasporic Brazilians in Europe or Cubans in North America. Jamaica's musical culture arguably experimented with music-making technologies in numerous ways that translated nicely in the global diasporic context. The ideas behind these experimentations, as King Tubby manually invented high-pass filters, echo and reverb, meant a culture of sonic experimentation could travel even without instruments and with any of the discarded or 'obsolete' technologies one could gather. In cities such as London or Toronto, one could continue experimenting with music making even without access to a local band and without a venue, recording studio or performance possibility.

The consistent tinkering and experimentation with mixing boards, turntables, microphones and speakers required little infrastructure to continue the kinds of cultural investigations into sound normalized in Jamaican musical culture. This culture, while intimately connected to technology, relied equally on audiences as music technology, so that in diasporic contexts the newly migrated Jamaicans in large numbers were critical factors for sound system success. The audience became the infrastructure in an interesting relationality that offset techno-determinist ideas of innovation. In this relationship between technology and people, the Jamaican sound system and the DJ become central figures in demonstrating how sonic Afro-modernity operates.

The chapters offered here represent an analysis and critique of our contemporary moment, beginning from a space opened up by Afrosonic innovations. *Afrosonic Life* imagines other versions of our present society, starting from the lived realities and embodied knowledge embedded in the ways music and sound are incorporated into Black life. The investment, as exemplified in a plethora of expressive cultural creations, has been in irreverent intertextual, interdisciplinary activities that remained both within the logic of Western modernity yet strategically 'played' with its excess. Black expressive cultures offer a creative praxis that provides openings to imagine, invent and operationalize ways of living beyond the reality constructed by European colonialism. Black creative praxis is opaque, offering refuge and pedagogy for a life that might speak to our present reality.

To give one example: when Kanye West rhymes on 'Jesus Walks', he 'defiantly' talks about 'God', inserting the religious song into his highly successful secular career. West's conjoining of the secular and the religious was a conscious effort. Within the track itself, West plays with the excesses of Western modernity by signalling how Afrodiasporic expressive cultures, as countercultures to modernity, refuse the isomorphic silos of Western thought. He rhymes, 'We ain't going nowhere but got suits 'n cases'. With this triple entendre, West points to how Afrosonic innovations, and expressive cultures in general, insist on a relationality that refuses and refutes a separation of the political, the economic and the social world. The social commentary embedded in these lyrics illuminates the limited, or lack of, social mobility for African Americans as the intensified growth of the prison-industrial complex ravages American life, even as West, infamous for his love of fashion, gestures towards the stylistic, with his shortening of 'lawsuits' into 'suits' cannot be lost on the listener. In ten words, West speaks to the social, aesthetic, political and economic realities of African American life – he does so in rhythm and on beat. Afrosonic innovations such as this triple entendre fuel the arguments and positionalities throughout this work.

Inside

The first chapter, 'Soundman/Sound System (S.W. rmx)', takes as its point of departure Wynter's new humanist oeuvre as central to exploring relational modes of being human. Throughout, an interrogation of the interface between Black folks as former commodities and the sonic technologies of today utilized by DJs challenge our present mode of thought. A mode of thought indebted to Western European enlightenment, which privileges the local knowledges from its continent, powerfully enforced by numerous colonial institutions. DJing, while demonstrating a wide variety of perspectives, is by and large focused on pleasure, joy and the securing of communal well-being through collaborative activities involving music. I spend time with Jamaican sound systems and the technique of the wheelback to move through the following questions, What is at stake if we are to take seriously Afrosonic innovations as ideological interventions into our present system of thought? The chapter suggests that the utilization of sonic technologies, such as the turntable, by former commodities operates through a conception of the human lived in excess of the dominant current conceptions of 'Man' as a purely biological being hierarchically arranged by race. What kinds of human modailities are proposed by sonic subjectivities?

Chapter 2, entitled 'Turning the Tables', focuses on turntablism as an example of the operation of an episteme that evidences a sonic subjectivity which diverges from dominant notions of 'Man'. The chapter explores the ideas, histories and the structures that made possible the art of turntablism and asks: how might this activity productively disrupt or rearrange our present systems of thought? The chapter also asks: what does turntablism tell us about our current conceptual itineraries around culture, Afrodiasporic sound, the relationship between human and machine? The chapter connects turntablism to Rastafari speech patterns to grapple with how the decommodifying techniques Turntablists demonstrate are connected to the counter-world embedded in the notion of I-and-I. My attention to language in this chapter functions to capture at the level of the everyday, how the creative strategies of wording the world provide possibilities for turntable experimentation and other sonic activities.

The following chapter, 'Riddim Science: On Living Hip-Hop's Sonic Innovations', brings together the riddim method found in reggaeton and Jamaican sound systems with DJ mixing practices found in hip-hop music. The chapter reads hip-hop's intertextual cultural aesthetics as a deciphering practice focusing on how mixtapes make use of and innovate around the riddim method to foreground repetition, difference and the seamless mix as an immaterial site of representation. This chapter makes the claim that the sonic innovations found on mixtapes are templates for a praxis for Black living in diasporic spaces. As with Chapter 2, I am attentive to all sounds audible to the human ear, as they are generative when not disentangled or isolated from other acts circulating in one's environment. Sonically, spatially and linguistically, the chapter details how riddim systems present a relationality that can form the basis for a lived praxis that departs from society's dominant discourses.

Chapter 4, 'Dubbing the Remix and its Uses', explores remixing, remix culture and its Jamaican ancestor, dub music. The chapter highlights the ways in which remix culture has disrupted consumer culture to explore the potential of a relational thought system indebted to the creative practices of remixing and its accompanying sonic subjectivity. Dub music anchors this chapter as remix culture's precursor, allowing for an exploration of the potential of the remix beyond copyright regimes. Inspired by dub engineers, I strip remix discourses of their obsession with copyright law and instead tune into the ways in which remixes offer up political possibilities and ways of decomposing and recomposing existing musical forms. This chapter captures echoes and reverberations of versioning and the 'cut 'n mix' mentality, examining the connections between these sonic interventions and thought processes related to the West African polyrhythmic practices of sound making.

In the concluding chapter, 'Come Again: We Were the First Robots', I briefly explore how the sonic innovations explored throughout point to the radical relational sonic subjectivities that structure how former African units of labour provide a glimpse of the multiple forms of being human.

1

Soundman/Sound System (S.W. rmx)

Music subverts the limits that are imposed on the Afro-Creole subject when reduced to 'symbolic Negro' within a code of objectification from the totality of his possibilities to a unit of labour within the capitalist paradigm of production.

—Wynter (cited in Mayseles 2002: 92)

Three short snapshots from the Afrosonic diaspora

Nineteen eighty-six, live at Union Square in New York, a seventeen-year-old emcee from Philadelphia implores the crowd to hear and observe the sounds his DJ invents on the turntable. DJ Jazzy Jeff proceeds, following direction from the other member of this duo, The Fresh Prince. Jeff is told to transform; he begins an arrangement of DJing techniques that involve rapidly moving the mixer's crossfader while slowly rubbing a recorded vinyl forward and backward at a speed, likely one-third slower than his other hand on the fader. We, the aural audience (listening at home on radio or cassette), and those physically present at the event have no idea what record is currently being transformed and this does not impact our enjoyment. At 3:32 in the routine, the crowd's roar confirms they at least appreciate, even if they cannot fully comprehend, what is happening on the turntables as Jazzy Jeff uses his hands to transform the vinyl into something sonically unrecognizable, at the edge of our intelligibility. The new sounds DJ Jazzy Jeff demonstrates with the transformer scratch, mimics the sound of the popular cartoon *The Transformers* and the emphatic crowd responses make clear that the prerecorded song on the vinyl he is using has greater value in its now defamiliarized state.

In Kingston, Jamaica, in 1967, sound system owner Ruddy Redwood is working in the studio with Duke Reid's engineer on cutting a record for an upcoming dance. The vocals of the Paragons' song 'On the Beach' are mistakenly left out of the recording. Redwood, rather than dwelling on this error, decides to bring a wordless rhythm track to his dancehall session. At the dance, the audience is pleasantly surprised to hear the vocals gone – they sing along, replacing the voices of the Paragons. Responding to their joy, Redwood's sound system extends this activity so that the song and the crowd participation on this song lasts somewhere between thirty minutes to an hour (Bradley 2000; Veal 2007).

In New York City, in the early 1970s, a teenaged DJ – an immigrant from Kingston, Jamaica – cannot get his audience to dance to his reggae music. He switches to funk music and, observing the increased intensity of dancers during the breakdown in each song, calls these dancers (including himself) break boys. This teenager, Clive Campbell, known as DJ Kool Herc, decides to continually repeat the break segment of these funk records by using two copies of the same record and repeatedly cueing the needle to the vocal-less breakdown of the record. He extends the break boys' favourite part of the song and extends their dancing pleasure. The verses and choruses on these records are disregarded in favour of the 'funkiest' section of the record – a wordless free-form departure from the song's structure (Chang 2005). This teenager thus gives birth to the breakbeat: a deconstructive innovation that becomes a core element of hip-hop and drum and bass music.

Introduction: B-sides of Western European modernity

These musical engagements are not 'normal' within the world of Western art music; they do not revere the score, they embrace improvisation and do not require existing forms of musical instrumentation or training. These musical engagements are prime examples of innovations at the core of sonic Afro-modernity. Each vignette demonstrates a relationality with its audiences via physically gathering, orally participating and sonically signifying on established musical norms. Continuously repeating the middle section of a song or rubbing a vinyl record back and forth until it becomes sonically unrecognizable resonates with very little from the traditions of Western art music. These innovations in sound do much to transform the record, from a commodity of consumerism into a tool of musical composition – each record's use value is elaborated beyond its market value. The invention of use value, as Sylvia Wynter reminds us in her essay 'Novel and History, Plot and Plantation' (1971), is one way in which Afrodiasporic populations simultaneously participate in the market while also resisting the totalizing effects of the market. Normal is a homogeneous set of behaviours Europe has circulated and regulated globally since the emergence of the printing press. Discourses of normality are not innocent; rather, they are invested with hegemonic power, systematically devaluing the unrecognizable. Normal, in relationship to Western art music, involves following a set pattern of notation, as well as being taught how to play a pre-existing instrument by a music 'teacher' and creating music (often) with cultural cachet or exchange value. The techniques of music making we find in Afrosonic innovations, such as dubbing, scratching, remixing and versioning, are not 'musical notions' taught or valued in Western art music. Rather, these 'not normal' techniques are critical interventions and innovations of the Afrosonic diaspora.

Wynter is instructive when she reminds us that there is

> always something else besides the dominant cultural logic going on and that something else constituted another but also transgressive ground of understanding ... not simply a sociodemographic location but the site both of a form of life and of possible critical intervention.
>
> (Wynter cited in Scott 2000)

Afrosonic innovations do not rest comfortably within the dominant cultural logic of Western societies, they are articulations of methods of Black life – ways to live beyond the strictures of the governing racial logic. Many sonic innovations, such as scratching a record, are illegible activities that cannot be read by the dominant logic as anything more than entertainment. The dominant logic – Western European thought – 'remains constrained by a theoretical apparatus generated by the practice of Atlantic slavery and its need to cast human relations as property relations' (Fischer 2015). These limitations mean a liberal humanist approach reproduces the social relations of its existence guaranteeing a linear narrative of freedom in one's escape from being property. Afrosonic innovations, imagined as forms of public nuisance and more recently commodified forms of entertainment, fit neatly into concepts of property that constrains how the theoretical possibilities of sound in the African diaspora might be understood.

Liberal humanism is a system of understanding of the human condition as one imbued with autonomy and the freedom to author one's life, history, meaning and actions. Given the inherent analytical problems of liberal humanism, it is fruitful to analyze sonic innovations in the African diaspora using Alexander Weheliye's notion of sonic Afro-modernity, and I examine more than the disjuncture between technology and Black life. More specifically, this project is attentive to the creative gap between the intended use of specific sound technologies and the 'misuse', or remixed use, of the turntable, mixing board and mixtape. The sonic as a 'transgressive ground of understanding' is critical in helping us grasp the other forms of logic, the other rationalities at work across the various sonic innovations I briefly outlined to open this chapter (Wynter 1992: 235). The constraints of Western thought have for too long obscured the forms of a subjectivity birthed by Afrosonic innovations that lay beyond the bourgeois ideal of secular Man. These innovations are experiments with sound that leverage generations of Afrodiasporic orality to actively subvert sound technologies as ways to displace the African as a technology of colonial capital accumulation – as a unit of labour. These innovations extend pleasure and Black joy in ways that are multisensory, opaque and which mitigate the biocentric nature of Europe's ocular obsession. In displacing the ocular as the central processing modality of Western human life, Afrosonic innovations foster possibilities of subjecthood that propose different ways to live as humans, a praxis that combines the ocular, kinaesthetic and sonic to creatively foster subjectivities often recalibrated in relation to 'Man'. The subjects created by sonic innovations are the 'something else', the 'more-than-Man' beyond the dominant disciplinary codes of our present order (Wynter 1992; Lowe and Manjara 2019). For these sonic subjectivities, intelligibility is not an end point; rather, a different set of metrics guide us beyond the idealized 'Man' formulation of the dominant code (Weheylie 2005: 68).

This chapter attends to the moments and methodologies embedded within sonic innovations that transform Man's 'other' from an object to a human subject. I am specifically interested in sonic matter that demonstrates an episteme, one invested in the development of tools and the subversion of sound technologies to enhance Black living. The sonic episteme evoked here is a system of knowing how to invent forms of Black living that divest of the labouring Black body, which signify on Western linear time, and that decommodify Black life through musical aesthetics and orality, which nullifies commodity status. These sonic innovations consistently subvert technology to prioritize the expression of Afrodiasporic aesthetics deeply entwined with an orality that privileges improvisation, repetition and call and response. These methods and techniques used to develop sonic subjectivities invent a modality through which Black life might enunciate a sense of 'ontological autonomy' beyond the racial schemas of the colonial enterprise (Wynter 1992).

In what follows, I explore techniques and expressions of Afrosonic innovations, bringing them into conversation with Sylvia Wynter's notion of Western 'Man' as an overrepresentation of the Human, to illuminate how Afrodiasporic forms exist beyond and remix the racial schemas of Europe's conception of 'Man'. Remix, in relation to music, involves for me a transformation through the addition and/or subtraction of elements through which familiarity and newness relationally redirect how we understand the original song. Extending this concept, my concern here is to understand another mode of being human that remixes the dominant concept of 'Man'. In this chapter, I examine two critical elements from which several sonic techniques are birthed, the turntable and the Jamaican sound system. The roles of sound systems and DJs are explored throughout, bringing into relation how technology, orality, sound and race are worked through in various mediums to produce a livable form of the human not overdetermined by dominant forms of 'Man'.

The demonic ground of sound: DJing as decipherment

For artists and critical consumers, music expresses and documents some of the most difficult aspects of human life, such as pain, heartbreak, racism and death. For colonial authorities, music produced by the 'wretched of the earth' was a synonym for rebellion; it posed the possibility of a social uprising.[1] Goat-skinned drums could communicate far and wide – their messages incomprehensible to some – triggering the outnumbered white planters to believe the music would incite rebellion, possibly signalling an end to their carefully constructed colonial social 'reality'. This 'reality' was one in which the non-European was discursively posited outside/beyond the limits of Christianity, a notion solidified by Caribbean and Latin American colonization. Drumming, as it was continuously outlawed across a number of colonies, such as Jamaica in 1792 and Trinidad in 1881, became the 'demonic ground', the area outside of the 'consolidated field of meanings' for colonial subjects (Wynter 1977: 207). According to geographer Clyde Woods, the 'act of making music parallel[s] an intellectual transformation', an often-overlooked aspect of Black musics (Woods 2007: 56). These overlooked sites, when carefully excavated, demonstrate how such intellectual transformations

---

[1] See Dudley (2003) on the various ordinances in colonial Trinidad, which attempted to ban multiple sound and musical experiences. The comments of many planters, such as Jamaica's Edward Long, briefly illuminate how the music of the enslaved was a constant trigger for white planters, amplifying their anxieties around potential rebellions.

from within the demonic ground of Afrosonic practices become productive arenas to explore other forms of human life, 'more-than-Man' formulations.[2]

Sylvia Wynter's main concern in her writings from the late 1980s onwards is to trace the development of Western bourgeois man as an overrepresentation of the category of 'human'. Wynter rightly asserts that Europe and whiteness 'is able to make itself into the biological norm of being as long as we continue to think of the human as a purely biological species' (Wynter 2006: 13). Wynter identifies two European constructions of Man (Man1 and Man2) that have come to represent the entire category of the human that arises as a result of this imposition of Western thought on non-European populations. Man1 was invented alongside Christianity; his orientation was religious and his encounters with non-Christians began constructions of the heathen. Man1 subscribed to a rigid and religious hierarchical chain of being model, placing himself above the savage brute but below perfect divine nature.

Man2, who developed almost concurrently, is the present conception of the human with which we are most familiar. Man2, secular, political and a state actor, developed alongside the rise of the biological sciences. During colonialism and the rise of Europe, Man2 reconfigured humanness by ideologically re-presenting himself as 'world' humanness. Man2 is biocentric, overinvested in his physical being, classifying the world according to the ideals of biological reasoning (of an ocular persuasion) and wealth. Thus, gender, race and sexuality are always produced as an excess, as an addition to the secular, universal Western bourgeois man. Biocentric man is detached, rational and autonomous, unencumbered by the Church and author of the 'violent classificatory systems' that attempt to organize the entire earth (McKittrick 2006).

Following Wynter's notion of 'demonic grounds', spaces where the minoritized, the racialized, the gendered and the impoverished dwell, such as the Caribbean, are where the underbelly or the B-side of modernity exists (Wynter 1990; Walcott 2006). Thinking through sonic innovations as expressions of sonic subjectivities helps to capture the diverse ways that Afrodiasporic populations formulate a praxis to navigate the racialization process and re-narrate their humanity in terms beyond simply phenotype. Such re-narration extends Afrodiasporic orality and is amplified in musical aesthetics telling us a different story about being human.

---

[2] See Lowe and Manjapra (2019) for their useful deployment of more-than-Man as a way to gesture towards the multiple forms of being human that lay before and beyond the recent colonial formations of Man.

If we revisit Sylvia Wynter's article, 'Jonkonnu in Jamaica: Towards the Interpretation of Folk Dance as a Cultural Process', she engages in a similar discussion around how Africans in the West humanized their landscapes. In her analysis of creolization and indigenization in the Caribbean, Wynter illuminates a notion of humanization that clearly articulates the centrality of African heritage and performative practices in the Americas. She notes, 'The African presence, on the other hand, "rehumanized Nature" and helped to save his own humanity against the constant onslaught of the plantation system by the creation of a folklore and folk-culture' (Wynter 1970: 36).

Here, Wynter highlights how Africans in the Americas existed adjacent to capital accumulation. She asserts, 'Folklore was the cultural guerilla resistance against the market economy' (Wynter 1970: 36). To speak of humanization, specifically by those individuals deemed chattel under colonialism, is to focus in on the creative process, the ways in which Africans in the Americas created alternative subjectivities and possibilities for living under particularly brutal conditions. Wynter is clear in her assessment of Black music as carrying a 'subversive consciousness' that can 'subvert the psychic repression' and present a counter-representation of reality (Wynter 1977: 896, 898). For Wynter, Black music is the site that evidences a sense of Black joy, expressed through enthusiastic responsive gestures and 'exhalation', where an 'uncolonized flow of desire' marks 'a liberation from normalized knowledge systems' (n.d.: 539). In a sense, one can imagine Black music as the soundtrack to the demonic ground of the 'Other' in that it can at times remain unintelligible as the 'language' of Black music operates outside of the realities of the dominant order.

This soundtrack is one in which the figure of the Selector/DJ plays a critical role in how sonic Afro-modernity interfaces with Black life. As Barbados court records show, the dance has been a primary site of socialization and plotting of rebellion for enslaved Africans, at least in the Caribbean, as far back as the 1700s.[3] In contemporary times, the dance remains an important site of socialization, but it is the Selector/DJ's intimate relationship to music and subversion of technology that maps new relations for Black life.[4] The dancehall and nightclub (in the colder metropoles of the Global North) become important sites in which labour, time and orality are interconnected to produce sonic subjectivities liberated

---

[3] See the important work of Jerome S. Handler (1982) on dances and the threat of insurrection within Barbados plantocracy.
[4] The limits of my study mean I cannot explore in its own right the important connections between music and dance.

(however temporarily) from the dominant culture of colonial and neocolonial Western European ideology. Selectors/DJs are at the centre of freeing (via dance) the body of its labour time. Various DJing techniques disrupt and rearrange Western linear time, while the dancehall is immersed in forms of oral culture that rehumanize Africans forcibly made into objects.

Sonic subjectivities beyond biocentric man

Using various techniques such as scratching, mixing and wheelbacks, DJs and Selectors[5] encourage their audiences to sing with the instrumental of their favourite song and to form another relationship with the song, as co-creators – not solely as consumptive subjects. These techniques continually interrupt the project of transforming humans into labouring objects and 'duped' consumers. The participatory nature of dancehall patrons and audiences (as Ruddy Redwood would discover playing the accidental version of 'On the Beach') creatively repositions these individuals as they move from audience to co-creator – demonstrating Hutton's notion of performance as social praxis and anticipating by several decades the co-authorship debates of remix culture (Diakopoulos et al. 2007; Hutton 2007: 129; Campbell 2009). As dancehall patrons creatively enter into a subjectivity that guarantees their agency as more than labouring bodies, the sound system and DJ also invent new relations to the vinyl recordings they manipulate. Various techniques of enlivening a dance, such as toasting (improvising) on the microphone, the repetition of a popular song and the mixing and remixing of records from various eras exemplify how DJs and sound systems become creative co-conspirators in the design of a unique sonic experience that dislodges the dominant logic of consuming publics. These acts refuse to see music as an object, but rather engage music as an ongoing co-creative effort (Butler 2014).

Repurposing discarded elements of colonial extraction such as oil drums and technological innovations such as the turntable, Afrodiasporic populations demonstrate a relational conception between sound and self. The sound system urges the labouring body to respond outside of market time while the turntable speaks eloquently of the potential of supposedly obsolete vinyl, the affordances of

---

[5] I identify the Selector as distinct from a DJ in the North American usage of the term, as a member of a reggae sound system. The DJ, the contemporary version of the radio disc jockey, is not part of a sound system, playing events in which they do not bring their own sound system.

analogue music making while interrupting strategic manufactured obsolescence practised by corporations.[6] DJs' and Selectors' creative use of the turntable contradict the manufacturer's clearly limited conception of their product. Turntables were made to play music, not make music. Yet, by developing a new relation to this sound technology, these agents of sonic innovation propose and co-author a praxis of relational humanity. In these sonic adventures, human and technology mutually leak into one another, countering our present mode of being by allowing for other sets of relations – other kinds of stories we can tell ourselves about being human in ways that exceed the social prescriptions of contemporary society.

DJs, Selectors, Turntablists, Dub Engineers and sound systems, when conceiving of themselves as related to a specific externalized entity such as sound, can and do alter and extend the usefulness of such an entity, evading the restrictions of the entity's socially prescribed use. Rather than technologize the human, these sonic engagements rehumanize the 'Other', not as ideal 'Man' but as a recalibration on a spectrum of modalities of being human. In technologizing the human, images of an increasing robotized voice are immediately conjured when we think of the use of audio tune in contemporary popular music (Weheliye 2017). The notion of technologizing the human often operates in the realm of a corrective with perfectionist tendencies. Rather than proceeding along such a potentially dehumanizing path (humans are error-filled entities), attention is paid here to how sonic innovations illuminate and amplify how the dehumanized and commodified Afrodiasporic individual articulates a sense of self that diverges from a dominant notion of Man as biologically overdetermined by race. Such rehumanizing efforts are born out of sonic innovations that provide a subjective knowledge base for the exploration of 'othered' kinds of humanness and human relations. For Afrosonic innovators, enlightenment might mean more than positing universal truths or the analysis of French philosophers and their texts. These sonic engagements suggest alternative avenues by which one might understand the human being of Afrodiasporic descent and all its ideological entanglements as something more than the ocular-centric Cartesian 'Man', or labouring tool of capital accumulation.

---

[6] The manufacturing of obsolescence is quite common in the commodification of music and the associated technologies to consume such music. The introduction of new formats to play music, from cassette to compact disc to MP3 file, are strategic in their attempts to maximize profit in the marketplace. This trend has become more visible in the production of DJ technologies in which versions of digital vinyl systems determine the use of specific kinds of hardware (mixers and controllers) one can utilize.

Afrosonic innovations, in their multisensory attentiveness, refuse to define humanness as solely a racialized labouring body. In revamping the use value of the turntable, the oil drum and other items, Afrosonic engagements articulate a system of being and knowing that brings into being a subjectivity and a multisensory consciousness, making it easier for us to glimpse other methods by which narrations and discourses of human life emerge that are both culturally and biologically interwined. For former commodities, such as the once enslaved African, these unconventional interactions with sound aid in the development of alternative modes of humanness. This mode of being human understands itself as coming into existence through the creation (poiesis) and reconstruction/ redefinition of sound and other sound-making activities. As an extension and substitute of the voice, Afrosonic engagements construct a mode of humanness through sound that posits and invents new relations. Voice and sound produce a narrative of humanness in which liberation is about the ability of one's creative acts to birth subjective knowledges that are necessary in the construction of alternative human futures. Within the dominant regimes of thought, freedom is understood as a legal right, something that requires a decree, documentation and perhaps other kinds of physical evidence. Sonic innovations allow us to view and perhaps live a sense of liberation in a slightly different rhythm, beyond the laws and letters of 'freedom'. A rhythm that brings together the Human as reinvented via sound – a sonic subjectivity and the lived reality of being racialized as Man's 'other'. This doubleness of humanness, one on a lower frequency, produces the possibility of living in a state of fluidity and agility to evade a totalizing and crushing social biocentric logic.

It is useful to build upon Katherine McKittrick's mapping of Wynter's generative Man overrepresented as the human argument. In her essay 'Axis Bold as Love', McKittrick maps the intersection of a Cartesian axis and a political spectrum to plot 'Man', Man's Other and a closed system where freedom is conceptualized within the terms of 'Man' (2015: 152). In McKittrick's formulation, it is a south-western quadrant of her diagram that is drawn up to identify the closed system in which the notion of freedom defined by Cartesian thought is never questioned. If we extend McKittrick's diagram and posit the fluid recalibrations of sonic subjectivities in both the north- and south-western quadrant, an exercise of plotting various sonic innovations captures how Afrosonic innovations continually recalibrate subjectivities in relation to both the market and the dominance discourses of 'Man'. In the northern quadrant, we might place those sonic innovations that are intelligible, such as formal music genres, to contemporary society. In the southern quadrant, a plotting of what I would call unintelligible sonic innovations, like the scratch or techniques like the wheelback, would help us imagine beyond the frame of reference of a society founded on Western European culture. If, indeed, artists and creative labour bring together the bios and mythos of human existence, plotting the calibrations of sonic subjectivities between Man's Other on the x-axis and the extension of left-wing political orientation on the y-axis illuminates the potential forms of human life that exist outside of the closed semantic system of liberal humanism.

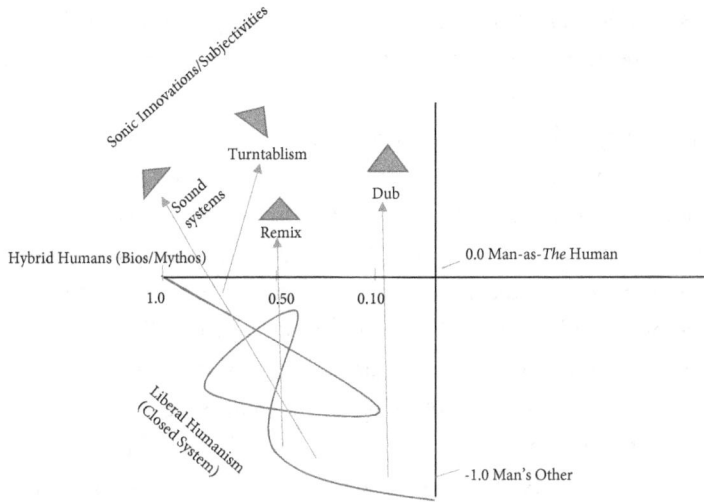

If position 0.0 on McKittrick's graph represents European 'Man' then positions -0.50, -7.0 and -14.00 moving to the left of the spectrum might signify a narrative beyond the limits of the stories of 'Man1' and 'Man2', both sonically invented and racially determined. The right quadrants here represent the hyperconservative market orientation, moving beyond a political orientation towards a neoliberal understanding of the human. Various factors influence the calibrations of sonic subjectivities, such as diaspora, migration and legal structures, which impact the duration and variety of one's diasporic reality. As McKittrick asserts, 'black creative texts move us beyond a purely biologized notion of the human' (2015: 160). Black musics, more specifically, are ethical sites for the recuperation and reimagination of the human, where one exists beyond the anti-Black present (Kamugisha 2016).

In understanding these innovations and Western 'Man' beyond the binary terms of the visual and to not reproduce the project of Western liberal thought,

Julian Henriques's conception of a sonic logos is helpful. Henriques asserts a triangular formation to move us away from the polarizing methods of European binaristic thinking. He outlines praxis, poiesis and episteme as nodes on his triangular formation, as a way of escaping the limits of racializing schemes and posing new questions about representational meaning beyond the visual. In Henriques's sonic logos, central is the episteme which considers that all knowledge can be loosened. Connected to this idea are acts of creation, poiesis and specific behaviours emanating from the episteme which contribute to sounding as a state of becoming (Henriques 2011). This triangular formation allows us to understand and maintain the relationality between specific technical practices, experiential knowledge and the forms of sonic creation that have fuelled popular music industries.

Extending beyond Black music, back to periods of enslavement, one might add rituals of repossession, secular-sacred expressions and masquerade performances, to the notion of 'performance as social praxis' – a necessary response to the conditions of enslavement (Hutton 2007: 129). These multiple modes of being human, one on an inaudible frequency beyond existing registers of bourgeois 'man', combined with the bare life of the flesh already inscribed in racial scripts, produces a doubleness of living in a state of fluidity and agility to evade a socially and economically inscribed, institutionally enforced, biocentric logic.

One way to evade the encasements of Western liberal humanism was, and is, to formulate specific existential practices, ways of self-fashioning, particularly for Afrodiasporic individuals, through sound and sound-making practices. Sonic innovations enable temporary moments in which subjectively 'free' beings emerge to form a knowledge base in which sonic subjectivities work to combine creative labour, oral culture and technological subversion to produce spaces outside of market time and racial schemas – ways of living a different kind of human. Within this knowledge base, improvisation, repetition and other oral and literary strategies loosen knowledge such that the dehumanizing practices of the colonial project and its current afterlife loosen their grasp on our subjecthoods (Gates 1988; Floyd 1996).

The performances of Afrosonic innovators are, then, more than solely commodities circulated for entertainment purposes; they are actions and activities in relation to their social conditions – texts, templates and paradigms for living Black life. In our contemporary context, in the afterlife of slavery, the machinations of late capitalism, neoliberalism and neocolonialism are frames that help us make sense of Afrosonic innovations. These coordinates are the empirical arrangements of any society that are 'inseparable' from the systems of knowledge and, thus, a necessary route to explore in order to disenchant existing arrangements of knowledge and power (Wynter 2006: 13). Accordingly, agents of Afrosonic innovations can be understood as 'ontological others ... [that] create innovative contributions to the de-objectification of a present system of theoretical absolutism' (Wynter 1992: 235). DJ performances, evidencing an ontological autonomy, gesture towards a social praxis yet to emerge at the level of discourse, one that not only refuses to be disciplined by the market but also dislodges the hegemony of visual schemas by relying on oral, aesthetic and kinaesthetic practices of Black living.

Moving through literature, philosophy and film, Wynter addresses the importance of cultural critique and the rewriting of our present episteme. She calls for a deciphering turn to avoid the kinds of cultural critique that do not interrupt our governing codes, and that instead juxtapose critiques from potent 'challenging' criticism – found in the work of authors such as George Lamming and films such as Spike Lee's *Do the Right Thing* (1989) – with those from what she calls a 'minority perspective' (Wynter 1992). Far from simply performing cultural criticism, Wynter argues for a deciphering practice conscious of its embeddedness within the 'cultural field of Western Europe' and interested in demystifying the process and procedures by which texts accomplish their work of reifying the prevailing codes of European thought (Wynter 1992).

The three sonic innovations used to open this chapter suggest a series of entanglements and innovations, which exceed Baker's (1984) African American blues matrix, as part of an episteme in which orality, refracted through music and other sonic innovations, continuously disrupts the colonial project of the invention and objectification of 'Others'. These entanglements and innovations belong within a series of musical gestures and aesthetics that include improvisation, repetition, hollers, blues notes, elisions, polyrhythms and more, usefully gathered under the rubric of 'Call and Response' by Samuel Floyd (1996). Sound technologies, such as sound systems and turntables, extend and evolve improvisation, repetition, call and response and the various other literary and oral inheritances from transatlantic life. Returning to Henriques's triangular formulation is useful here, amplifying the rationalities attached to acoustic and sonic space towards a notion of Afrodiasporic rationality that is multisensory, taking the visual and the sonic as multiple nodes from which to understand and articulate human life. My focus on DJing and by extension the sound system, embraced as an underappreciated institution central to Black diasporic life, is meant to move us beyond an American-centric blues matrix as we continue to grapple with the role of technology in Black diasporic musics (Chude-Sokei 1994).

Sound Systems as soundsystems

In Jamaica, travelling sound systems of high-fidelity speakers and amplifiers gained popularity in the country's urban centres in the 1950s and eventually began displacing big bands as more efficient and affordable musical entertainers. Jamaican sound systems have been the site of various oral, musical and sonic experimentations (Bradley 2000; Hutton 2007; Veal 2007). They showcase how Jamaicans engaged with sound technologies rather than passively accepting the limitations imposed by either the unaffordability of live bands or the stasis of sound equipment imported onto the island (Bradley 2000; Hutton 2007). As sound systems evolved, specialized roles emerged so that the owner of the sound system would have an Engineer to manage the sound quality, a Selector to change records and a DeeJay whose job became microphone control and audience entertainment. It is interesting to note the diasporic entanglement in which the African American disc jockey, whose powerful radio signals reached the Caribbean basin, influenced the development of the kinds of oral acrobatics that DeeJays like U-Roy employed. In an ironic twist, the sound system aesthetics DJ Kool Herc employed, as a Jamaican migrant to New York, with his massive bass-filled speakers did not replicate the sound system structure; he billed himself as an individual, not as a collaborative entity.[7] As we know, in the American context the term disc jockey remains closely tied to the musical rather than the oral aspects of dances and parties.

When the United States closed its doors to Jamaican migrant labourers, the flow of southern American soul music vinyl records also ended. Jamaican popular music consequently became more enterprising, looking instead to produce records to satisfy the local market for music. The accidental recording of an instrumental backing on a separate track (outlined to open this chapter) led to the creation of the vinyl-recorded instrumental version on the B-side

---

[7] The Herculords appeared on flyers, at times as DJ Kool Herc and the Herculords; they consisted of several emcees, Coke La Rock, Timmy Tim, Herc, Clark Kent, LeBrew and Imperial JC (see 'The Third Place, Mar. 6, 1981' 1981). Regardless, even at the level of naming, Herc, Grandmaster Flash and Afrika Bambaatta did not completely replicate the structure of Jamaican sound systems, even if aspects like toasting evolved into emceeing.

of records (Bradley 2000; Barrow and Dalton 2004). This curious accident enhanced the sonic artillery of the sound system, as invigorated dancers added the words to the instrumental backings of their favourite songs. The recording of instrumentals on the B-side of records operated as an economic imperative for producers to maximize profit, while simultaneously opening up the music scene to greater opportunities to experiment with audio recording (Veal 2007; Howard 2016). The B-side created the possibility of new space for experimental music making that did not need to fit the anticipated songs advertised on the A-side of records. It was not uncommon for a Selector to follow a very popular tune with the instrumental track in which dance hall participants respond to the instrumental version by singing aloud the lyrics to the song. This moment was eventually encouraged by dancers shouting 'version' in the midst of a song, hailing the Selector to play the B-side instrumental version of the song (Bradley 2000; Veal 2007).

In these moments when the dancing audience calls out 'version' to signal their pleasure to the sound system, the overrepresentation of Man as the ideal mode of being human becomes exposed as a contextual and culturally sanctioned position when Kingstonian dance hall attendees and British subjects (until 1962) refused to subscribe to the rigid Cartesian Man2 model. When the Selector fades out the lyrics and audiences perform themselves into the existing structure of the instrumental song, their co-creative actions move them from consumptive subject to a participatory subjectivity. In this moment, the sound system provides a possibility of rehumanization, a reordering of sound that displaces the racialized schemas as the dominant modality of subject making/hood. Those dancing and singing along exit the condemned status of labouring Black body, 'Man's other as invented by colonial Europe. In this process, the DJ and sound system create an environment in which the act of versioning loosens the authoritative grasp of normative 'Man' by performing a narrative of being human that pivots on call and response, repetition and improvisation within the music and the prioritization of the sonic.

The work of B-side versioning interrupts the dominance of Cartesian discourses, which constructed a binary between intellectual and bodily expression – the classificatory system that distinguished static recorded song from animate living person. Aesthetically, delight and joy within Afrosonic practices was not recorded as a detached process. Instead, the delight was enacted through participation within the very structure of the performance, an interruption and humanization of the song as well as its decommodification.

Such an intellectual transformation involves a reconceptualization of self through the music, outside of the formalized legal and social structures of society. This transformation signals the emergence of a sonic subjectivity, an operational modality informed by sound, music and oral culture – one that mitigates the ocular-centric racial schema already reinforced by society's institutions. Dance hall attendees in the Jamaican sound system scenario, situated as consumers of a record and positioned on demonic ground as racialized Man's other, improvised a new relationship to the record and the sound system via numerous Black musical aesthetics, from polyrhythms, call and response, wheelbacks and other forms of sonic significations. These responses to improvised lyrics to the record, instrumental tracks and one's favourite song transform the consumer producer binary and exceed efforts to contain the Black labouring body whose immediate responses of dancing and singing are rhythmically outside of market time and unprofitable to colonial institutions. At this moment of communal lyrical response, as the B-side instrumental record is actively redesigned in a participatory fashion, the song becomes the embodiment of a new mode of narration in which the hybrid human remerges as Black musical aesthetics structure the human differently, within a lineage of Afrodiasporic orality that is not reliant on racial formations.

The act of versioning not only decentres the central component of commercial music commodities – the lyrics of a song – but it also calls into question the status of the periphery and the margins, in the consumer/producer binary. The very authority of the centre, in this case the lyrics of a recorded song as evidence of the song's hermetically sealed autonomy, is replaced by the desires of the excess of modernity, the non-European, the poor, the formerly enslaved, the otherized. In the active performance of versioning live in a dancehall setting those deemed as the consumer, the labourer or one without the means of production replace the idealized centre – the artist chosen to sing the song (whose labour is commoditized). This moment is not just one of voicing or the subaltern speaking, it is one in which the deselected 'other' exits labour time and centralizes oneself as a creative agent co-producing (with the sound system) a moment in which their audibility is front and centre, either collaborating with or displacing the primacy of the musical commodity. The dancing body and singing voice exit racializing schemas and evade the extractive logic that imagines them as units of labour (and eventually consumers) to rewrite a narrative of living filled with endorphins, strained vocal cords and beads of sweat in the service of joy and the audibility of sounds that mark one a non-object, as human.

Here, it is important to notice the role of the technologies and commodities of being 'modern': the 2-track recorder in Duke Reid's studio that the engineer accidentally recorded an instrumental onto; the vinyl records imported to Jamaica by farm labourers; the discarded oil drums from Trinidad's emergence in the oil industry (Dudley 2003; Veal 2007: 52). The relationship between Afrosonic innovations and sound technologies is an important nexus in the articulation of a sonic episteme.

The Jamaican sound system remains a critical catalyst in sonic Afro-modernity, home to and channelling a variety of oral aesthetics via sonic innovations. These innovations remain staples in both the electronic music industry as well as in the Caribbean music ecosystem more than half a century since their inception (Veal 2007). What do these and other sonic innovations, when filtered through technological mediums, tell us about the process of rehumanization? If we consider that these musics are 'not limited to the technological complex in which [they] originated', then we need not limit our analysis to the confines of musical theory, colonial legal systems or capitalist modes of overproduction and manufactured obsolescence (Gilroy 1991: 128).

Having birthed the DeeJay, dubplate, specials and continued traditions of call and response and improvisation, the sound system has indeed been a cultural institution (Chude-Sokei 1994). Lyrical improvisations by sound system emcees, known as DeeJays in Jamaican parlance, sprung out of the sound system, paving the way for today's emcees found in hip-hop and jungle music. The earliest toasters, such as Count Machuki and King Stitt, and others became not just masters of ceremony but critical elements in the stylistic development of sound systems (Hutton 2007). That their lyrical innovations were filtered through (at times makeshift!) microphones, mixers and a dynamic arrangement of speakers signals a relational sonic Afro-modernity. In this relationship to the modern, the gap between a technology's intended use and its misuse value is initiated by the ways the voice brings legacies of Afrodiasporic orality to bear on the latest piece of music technology. Afrosonic innovations inscribe a use value that erodes exchange value, decommoditizing music and decommodifying sound.

The main job of the Selector/DJ is to ensure their audiences dance continuously and enjoy themselves. Such a task includes measuring the level of enjoyment of each song via call and response; digging for tracks that people may not know but might want to dance to; and creating a continuous flow of sound that encourages people to communicate their appreciation for such sounds through dancing and emphatic oral responses. Great DJs are known as those who practice a certain sensitivity to their audience's emotions, a 'musical editor' (Brewster and Broughton 2006) who participates in the emotionscape of the dance. This might mean cutting to the 'funkiest part' of the record as DJ Kool Herc did for the break boys dancing at his parties or this might mean extending a song by looping segments of the track as Tom Moulton and Frankie Knuckles famously accomplished in the disco and house. Such musical editing is always orientated towards inducing pleasure by prioritizing dancing patrons, sometimes with commercial benefit when it came to cutting new remix records or new dub versions.

Outside of the Jamaican dance hall, as we see with various DJ innovations in multiple musical genres, DJing is not just about cultural gatekeeping and tastemaking but is also a site of experimentation. DJs make possible the grounds to refute the bourgeoisie ideals of self-comportment, Western linear time and the labouring Black body to exceed the value schemas rigidly attached to race, when they create environments of joy, pleasure and escape even while regularly violating copyright regimes. A deciphering turn approach to DJ techniques illuminates the governing logics of consumption, designed to be a unidirectional experience yet exploded by the DJ's techniques and experimentations. DJs and sound systems induce sound as a tool of identification that operates around property, racialization and coloniality, using sound-making technologies to extend various aspects of Afrodiasporic orality – arguably one of the few tools Africans in diaspora could regularly deploy to interrupt their objectification. In recalibrating the ocular logics of white supremacy, DJs' innovations can be thought of as instigators of alternatives to the rigidity of musical genres, linear time and Western art music.

The Selector/DJ stands at this important intersection between sound technologies and Afrodiasporic innovations, shaping new ways to continue the project of liberation as unfreedom continues to characterize the colonial enterprise. The Selector/DJ uses various devices such as turntables, samplers and drum machines to enunciate, refashion or remap the social location of Blackness – that disjuncture between social perception and subjective understanding/reality (Moten 2003). The DJ interacts in an unmediated fashion with the turntable, in control of a stylus and needle whose job it is to extract sound from acetate or vinyl. While DJing the Selector/DJ is trapped in a nexus of having to please their audiences, while having to utilize their particular sound technology to achieve this goal. There exist two conversations at this moment, one with a machine that determines the next conversation which is with the audience. The second conversation is the Selector/DJ's use of their hands to intervene on the playing record, choosing which part to repeat, which words or sounds to emphasize and where to add reverb or echo. This second conversation can easily lead to a ravaging of the familiarity of any given record as the Selector/DJ utilizes several techniques to enhance the sonic experience.

As a creative agent in the sounds that emanate from a vinyl source, the Selector/DJ violates the 'authority' of the record, not only suggesting other ways or narratives to sonically/aurally experience the record – and by extension our social reality – but also materializing them. A record's authority is derived partially from its form as a manufactured piece of vinyl and partially through the kinds of copyright legislation that limit how consumers interact with the industry's commodity forms. The continual subversion of electronic sound technologies, from the sampler to the drum machine, expresses a cognitive autonomy that seeks to exceed the function of objects such that these objects are given voice – the ability to articulate another function of their form. The ideas that encourage a DJ to spin the record backwards, make thinkable the isolation of a breakbeat or the mixture of different records into one soundscape are the ideas of this muted conversation between technological commodity and former commodity. Do various forms of sound technology induce new processes of thought? Can sound technologies speak for, or extend the 'voice' of, the formerly enslaved? With these questions in mind, I am interested in teasing out the sonic utterances (wheelbacks, screams, scratches), suggestions or demands of an alternative understanding of how peoples, ideas or positioning within the African diaspora are, or can be connected to, revamping our present 'modes of truth' in light of the multiple realities of our present. Thinking through the turntable's sonic innovations illuminates how technologies of sound are utilized to move from object to a subjectivity based in the sonic. Afrosonic innovations – as sources of delegitimized forms of knowing and living that cannot enter our present system of knowledge – hold the potential to amplify the relationality proposed beyond biocentric man. One technique in particular, the wheelback, is an ideal way to further dive into the sonic epistemic intimacies of DJing.

The wheelback

The DeeJay in Jamaican sound system culture is the person who controls the microphone during an event, vocalizing various kinds of information and entertainment for the attendees. DeeJays reformat the sound of records through vocal interruptions and a Selector uses a technique of manually rewinding the record, what I will refer to as the wheelback. Like the Turntablist, DJs and Selectors participate in the event of sound making by interrupting the record while it is playing. The DeeJay toasts on the record, providing improvised vocal sounds, continuously interrupting the record that is playing to endorse the sound system's prowess, the crowd's energy or the track playing. During these interruptions, the DeeJay turns down the sound of the record playing and speaks their mind over the record. The early innovators in this regard, such as Vincent 'Duke Vin' Forbes, Leroy 'Cuttin's' Cole and Red Hopeton, elaborated a number of oral 'gestures' such as wisecracks and short rhymes over the music provided by the sound system (Hutton 2007).

The additional sounds provided by these DeeJays included rhymes, humorous stories and, eventually, in a later period, the mimicking of gunshots and other verbal sounds and words. For instance, at a dance that took place June 2006 involving two of Jamaica's biggest sound systems, Stone Love and Bass Odyssey, the DeeJay took the liberty of inciting people to shout out their support for the sound system only if 'them never kill baby', 'if them nah rape' (track 2 1:06) or if they 'love dem Muddah' (track 17 1:39). In these continuous interruptions of the record, the DeeJay inserts themself into the record, the event of sound making becomes more equalitarian, involving interruption and call and response tactics in a way that suggests one can co-create alongside a musical commodity. So when the DeeJay calls out to the audience to respond if they 'love dem Muddah', encouraging them to put their hands up or wave a lighter, this call and response concurrently operates within relation to the theme of the track playing. At this point in the event, Bass Odyssey prepares to play its final song, the Boyz II Men track, 'A Song for Mama'. The DeeJay's frequent interruptions also decentre the song, with the crossfader (or volume knob) being used to mute the music at different times. The DeeJay's voice works in tandem with the Selector's crossfading, and at times they work together to synchronize their timing, inserting themselves out of time with the playing record.

Such sound thinking involves understanding a certain relationship between the individual and the record, thinking of sound as something connected to the social space, another area for subjective representation. Thus, for the toasting Jamaican DeeJay, their sonic subjectivity transforms the prerecorded sound into a public conversation, one that can be interrupted and agreed with such that ad libs that have now become canon in the Jamaican dancehall scene are often explosive affirmations such as the extended and heavily bass filled

'Riiiiiiggghhhhht' associated with Stone Love sound system in the 1980s and 1990s. In the June 2006 party, the DeeJay's consistent interruptions produce a dissonance both sonically and in terms of timing, as only one instance occurs when the DeeJay decides to ride the rhythm of the track playing (track 2 0:45). The DeeJay's gruff voice is in no neat sonic relation to the variety of songs played by the system; the voice is a much lower tone and either matches or exceeds the intensity of the song. Vocal harmony by the DeeJay does not appear to be a valued aspect of the voicing process – the lower register of the voice is consistently out of tune with many of the songs interrupted.

In these public conversations, such as this 2006 beach party, the voice is given primacy, often interrupting the song using an off-beat insertion. This voice is a class-based interruption into public discourse and public space, as Jamaica's Uptown–Downtown class divide remains rigid since mass urbanization in the late 1950s and 1960s.[8] In the DeeJay's toasting early in the set, the audience is privy to notions of anti-abortion and anti-rape sentiments, mixed with residues of hypermasculinity and the objectification of women. There is a refusal to play upper-class respectability politics, one that runs rife throughout Jamaica's social and political arenas. The voice that is made to interrupt the record is also made to interrupt the mutability of a lower-class sentiment often ignored or chastised by the dominant culture (see Stolzoff 2002; Cooper 2004; Stanley-Niah 2009). In one interesting moment at the June beach party, a woman from the audience can be heard mimicking the DeeJay's phrasing to denounce fathers that don't take care of their children (track 18 1:23). Instead of repeating or ignoring the woman's gripe on the microphone, after chuckling to himself, the DeeJay rephrases her contention into an exultation on the microphone to big up the good fathers and men who take care of their children. The layers and levels of relationality are multiple and complex as gender, class, geography and sound intersect in milliseconds producing no neat or linear connection to the ruling class's ideological desire to reproduce bourgeois culture. The seemingly democratic space of the call and response is regulated by the DeeJay whose job is to control the mood of the event. Yet, the audience member's public discussion

---

[8] Prior to political independence from Britain in 1962, Jamaica experienced mass urbanization, with rural populations flocking to the country's capital city seeking employment and opportunity. The Uptown–Downtown divide in the city is one that bears both racial and class tensions, as colour correlated with class, Uptown has been home to the middle classes more closely aligned with bourgeoise values. Downtown Kingston has been home to nightclubs and the very rich reggae music scene, often seen in direct contrast to Uptown.

of domestic affairs tells us something about where they imagine public discourse is possible, safe or necessary for those whose family structures do not reflect the hegemonically dominant nuclear model. The DeeJay's decision to rephrase the woman's complaint and her words confirms the audience member's belief in the dance as a safe space, and his rephrasing possibly indicates his attempts to ensure the right vibe, via an absence of anger, to ensure the event has proper vibes.

Alongside the various ways in which the voice is made to interrupt a playing record, the Selector's technique of rewinding the record adds an additional layer of sound, often in a register that stands in stark contrast to the bass heavy design of the sound system. This moment of the wheelback is when a record is played and then manually rotated backwards and set to the beginning of the track, often at the height of the exuberant responses and cheers from the dancing audiences. The wheelback operates in at least two ways: as a responsive gesture when audiences demonstrate a heightened appreciation or euphoric sentiment and as a tool for creating hype.

As a technique, the wheelback can involve either the lifting of the stylus and the placing of it to the first groove in the record or the manual anticlockwise rewinding of the record with the Selector's hands. There is a physicality to this counter-rotation wheelback of the seemingly linear and progressive rotation of a recorded vinyl, a demonstration of skill that audiences can sometimes witness visually. Its affective impact is the garnering of voluminous oral responses from the audience, which might call out 'version' in the 1960s, 'dubwise' in the 1970s or emulate the sounds and gestures of gunshots in the air in reference to the reported activities of former policeman turned sound system owner Duke Reid, who was known to let his pistol off during dances. Alternatively, the wheelback might be called for by the DeeJay so that *'lick it back to the top!'* or *'pull up dat and play back'* might be heard by the Selector as instructions for them to try and *'toy with audience expectations'* (Veal 2007: 75). Early in the dance, Bass Odyssey performs three wheelbacks not in response to the crowd (track 2 0:15). Rather than performing the wheelback at the height of the dance in response to crowd reaction, Bass Odyssey utilizes it early on to enhance the vibes and increase the excitement of the event. Depending on the medium of the sound and the preference of each sound system, the distorted backwards sound of a song may or may not be let out by the crossfader for the audience to hear, possibly connected to the timing within the duration of the dance.

The DeeJay's commands might follow the crowd's physical/bodily response to the record or in the example provided here with Stone Love and Bass Odyssey, the wheelback gets utilized to provide a space to 'chat on the mic' rather than in specific reaction to the crowd responses. As the stylus amplifies the tune, the Selector/DJ and possibly the sound system owner peer out at the crowd. In this moment of repeating a new or already popular song, the sound system enters into relation with the expectations of the dancehall patrons. The audience's reactions are carefully observed, the possible success of a track lies in the response of the dancers, the sound system calls for a participatory, expressive and instantaneous relation to the record being played.

Frequently, when audiences call out for a 'pull up' – indicating a desire for the Selector to wheelback the song – the chronology of musical events is interrupted long before the track has reached its end. In this scenario, the linear musical experience appears to have no value, a paradigm of interactivity, of call and response in an improvisational manner appear to matter more. As Henriques points out, standing in stark contrast to the protest and work ethic and linear notions of progress, the repeating moment of the wheelback reflects a broadly African musical sensibility (2011). With an emphasis on rhythm and timbre, its antiphonal structure, rhythmic contrast and the collective social experience, the moment of the wheelback fits nicely into composer Olly Wilson's 'heterogenous sound ideal' (1992) and James Snead's focus on the 'cut' in Black musical cultures (1981). The wheelback allows for a cut to the existing song, such that a gap of silence in which no music is being played opens up to the crowd's cheers. This pocket of no music in which audience voices dominate the soundscape, is a location of joy – a Black joy induced by sound and devoid of the dominance of the visual.

Within the Jamaican music ecosystem, it was regular practice to record a song, cut it to an inexpensive acetate and test out the track with audiences in a dancehall that same day or week. This method of testing the market relied on the development of a relation between the music, the sound system and the dancing patrons. For songs that struck a chord with audiences, it was not uncommon for one song to play multiple times at a dance or play for an extended period of time. The multiple calls for a wheelback from the audience were directly related to not only the promotional plan for each new song but also the pleasure of dancing patrons in an exit of market time and the labouring Black body.

Much like the amplifier feedback Jimi Hendrix transformed into a musical experience, the moment of the wheelback crafted new (and desirable) sonic relations dominated by repetition, familiarity and the emergence of a new sound. The record being manually turned backwards creates an incomprehensible sound, it disrupts the listener's pleasure at the same moment that it enhances and intensifies the listening experience with its high-pitched screech. Euphoria is extended as the abundance of bass vibrating through the air is sliced through with the squealing timbre of the rapidly backwards moving vinyl or the modern-day steel platter we find on today's digital controllers. No words or sounds are decipherable, yet in this moment of immense pleasure, the refusal of the track's linearity and the maximizing of audience's insistence on enjoying the repetition of the track speaks volumes. Time is made to stand still in the moment of the wheelback and the record's return to the beginning of the track. The future is then composed from a repetition of a past. Market time, the efficiency of the West's hyper obsession with profit, is made to yield to the consciously extended moment of Black joy. With gunfingers in the air, lighters, handkerchiefs or anything else, the physical and oral response of the crowd reverberates across the dance hall; it becomes the dominant soundscape of this temporary musicless moment made possible by the intimate intersection of improvisatory toasting, mastery of timing and the embrace of the towering house of joy speakers.

The unrecognizability of the song during the wheelback, its backwards words, its imprecise and shifting velocities and its improvised yet relational timing become a poignant reminder of levels of opacity embedded in an Afrosonic innovation bursting with various vestiges of musical aesthetics and residues of orality. Yet, for the many levels of sonic and oral inventiveness in the wheelback, a constitutive element of this sonic practice remains the people in relation. The response to the song is also a call for repetition, not just an extension on non-market time, but an extension and manual repeating of joy. The voice momentarily overtakes the new space created by the wheelback, scattered calls, shrieks and whistles burst forth from the crowd filling up this out of time geography. A polyphonic soundscape emerges in which the music is only one of many competing sounds and where the human voice, interrupting its objectification, signifies on Western linear time and the over-consumptive, yet exalted, human modality.

In this moment of relationality, there is a reliance on one another – not just of the audience's response to the record but also of the shift in energy from sound system to audience and back again. The wheelback functions on multiple registers and frequencies to disrupt the labour time of the Black diasporic (post) colonial subject and the accompanying visual subjection (Weheliye 2005). 'Man' is decentred in this moment, another relation is managed in which the record, body, time and sound diffuse the crushing weight of colonial conceptions of being of its appeal or potency. Rational Cartesian 'Man' invested in a mind–body split takes a back seat to the desire for joy and the hegemonic ideals around comportment and progress, in their European colonial formation, ceases – time is now under the control of the masses, the DeeJay and the Selector. The existing colonial language of progress is placed in question, the empowered masses increase definitional ambivalence around 'progress' and place primacy on the immediate pocket of joy invented by this sonic innovation. With time controlled, the refusal to reify existing arrangements becomes a possibility – a different future can be imagined and enacted. The oral and immaterial, refracted through sound-making technologies, emerge as an assemblage of repetition, with a call and response and improvisation inviting the crowd to explore and exceed the limited form of the fixedness of the vinyl recording, the popular song format and, by extension, the proposed comportment of music consumers and (neo) colonial subjects. Communal experience upends desires of individual ownership of the tune and the ephemerality of dancing to the tune is emphatically disrupted by the repetition of the record called for in the moment's call and response, wheelback or 'pull up' demanded by the crowd. Each repetition of the song allows for another reiteration of the dancing audience member's individual ownership of their body with improvised movements in the service of joy, not profit. Music as an object is obliterated at this moment.

The sound system enters an intimate relationship with the expectations of the audience members. Knowledge of the forthcoming pleasure of a track is controlled and repeated by the Selector – labour time is actively and repeatedly disregarded. The Selector uses their control of the record. The call and response here is multidirectional – the Selector's wheelback calls for dancehall participants to 'free up', that is, shrug off their worries and eliminate the stressors of the past and present. Dancing patrons respond with vigorous applause, dancing and oral cues of approval and emphatic delight. In controlling the mood of the dance, the Selector, in combination with cues from the DeeJay, induces sonic subjectivities, whose reliance on orality disrupts the primacy of the visual and racial schemas. The kinaesthetic, oral and aural are combined to forge a new set of relations, one in which Afrosonic aesthetic practices are central.

The wheelback, in its insistence on a radical relationality between linearity, improvisation and call and response provides a frame for DJs, turntablism and the deciphering activities of Afrosonic innovations channelled through the turntable, mixing board or microphone. The subjective modes produced by these technological engagements amplify how sonic Afro-modernity houses alternative, adjacent identities and subjectivities. This is precisely the moment where liberation is imagined and articulated beyond the language of freedom.

Other(ed) kinds of humans

The breakbeat is a form of music making that involves utilizing samples of portions of records to create a continuous repeating loop of sounds. Today, the excessively sampled tracks James Brown's 'Funky Drummer' and the Winston's 'Amen Brother' form the backbone of several musical genres including dubstep, drum and bass, garage, hip-hop and Big beat. The breakbeat is a core part of electronic music today. When DJ Kool Herc first isolated the breakbeat in the early 1970s, he was exemplifying the fundamental connection of the African diaspora to a notion of liberation as a non-linear, participatory and creative activity. Herc would utilize two of the same records and move the needle to the breakdown section of each record, rarely beginning at the start of the record. For the Winston's 'Amen Brother' around the 1:26 mark, the horns drop out and it is just the bass and drums that produce the funkiest part of the record. DJ Kool Herc would continue to repeat just this section of the song several times to align with the dancing energies of the break boys, those eventually called breakdancers. To continuously repeat the breakbeat section of records meant the DJ participated both physically and sonically in reordering the sonic arrangement. Herc's innovation was deeply relational, a site where call and response and improvisation utilized visual, sonic and kinaesthetic engagement to please the crowd.

Thinking through sonic innovations alongside Wynter's project to find an emancipatory breach in European Man overrepresented as the Human allows us to engage a narrative of being human not entangled within the semantic trap of liberal humanism. The kinds of music-making practices detailed throughout this chapter operate as landscapes of knowing and being that suggest a subjectivity that exists beyond the intelligibility of a Cartesian reference point. From Aunt Hester's scream that Fred Moten attends to in *In the Break* to the wheelback examined in this project, intelligibility within our current regime of knowledge is not a precursor to the work sonic innovations might accomplish. The examples of sonic subjectivities we find authorized by Negro spirituals (mentioned in the introduction) or the Turntablist (elaborated in the following chapter) allow us to recognize a narrative of being human filtered through both analogue and digital sonic technologies, yet firmly embedded in a lineage of Afrodiasporic orality and musical aesthetics. For the singer of a 'Wade in the Water', their praxis of being human was immediately concerned with mitigating the impacts of a racialized schema, using the voice as a technology to map new geographies. For the hip-hop producer, their uses of digital technology express a subjective knowledge about the merits of an approach to technological subversion invested in a relationality such that the humanizing of drum programming, popularized by the late J. Dilla, is a celebrated sonic innovation. The humanizing of electronic drum kits by J. Dilla's refusal to quantize his drums mirrors the Selector and DJ's refusal to play records in a linear fashion, allowing for the interruptive pleasures of the audience to rehumanize each (commoditized) song's affective impact in real time. A multisensory approach, adding sonic rationality and kinaesthetic activity to an ocular bias regime of colonial discourse interrupts the silence of Plato's cave, presenting an approach to being human that operationalizes itself through three sensory avenues (Henriques 2011).

Given the illegal conditions under which enslaved populations sought Western literacy, as well as the outlawing of the drum in several colonies, there existed very few possibilities for Other Humans to enter the discursive terrain of 'Western Man' other than as non-humans. Consequently, the processes of 'thingification', as a humanity-stripping transformation to create subjugated populations, actively sought to destroy the avenues through which enslaved populations made sense of their world (Césaire 1972: 42). The tenets of modernity and the rigid requirements of 'enlightened perspectives' policed the covert performative and sonic expression that enslaved populations in the West used to negotiate and invent a hybrid approach to being human in their lives – a sonic mitigation of visual schemas.

As Wynter unravels Man1 and Man2, shrouded in notions of autonomy, progress and freedom, it is clear these conceptions cannot contain the sonic and performative practices of formerly enslaved Africans. 'Thingification' situates for us the centrality of creative (sonic) acts – a critical aestheticism that forms a knowledge base from which personhood is forged: a knowledge base by which 'things' mobilize to become 'humans' or subjects. Césaire's signal towards a 'science of the word' points us in the direction of the centrality of creative acts in the survival and articulation of post-Middle Passage Black life (McKittrick 2021).

Afrosonic innovations are, then, ways to remix European conceptions of 'Man' through creatively mixing sonic, oral and kinaesthetic practices with and against existing racialized schemas. Although never replacing the dominance of Eurocentricism with its ocular-obsessed racial hierarchy, these Afrosonic innovations produce varied results and new narratives that are biologically informed – as the physicality of music making is significant – and culturally embedded both within generations of orality and musical aesthetics, and adjacent to the music industry. Afrosonic innovations disrupt notions of autonomy and authorship troubling the Eurocentric underpinnings of contemporary Western cultural production. Central to this praxis for living Black life is the opacity of sonic innovations. The intelligibility of these forms of knowledge is always in question, such that the dub innovations of Lee Scratch Perry or DJ Jazzy Jeff's transformer scratch point to the outer limits of the dominant regime's discursive hegemony towards a sonic subjectivity that is not market oriented and that is largely indifferent to Western notions of taste. Thus, the sonic subjectivities fostered by Afrosonic innovations design ways of knowing oneself that do not accept the validity of a racializing schema, instead inventing and recalibrating a positionality that might mitigate structures of domination.

By remixing a narrative of being human, sonic innovations gesture at conceptions of human life attuned to and in tune with the rhythms of Black life – rhythms that are cognizant of the harm of anti-Black racial hierarchies and which work to undo them. The participatory structures of Afrosonic innovations do not privilege a biocentric version of being human; instead, they explore a relationality between human and technology/machine, between time and movement and between the sonic and the visual to create insurrectionary forms of knowledge and culture that refuse to accept the logic of biocentric humanness. As such these innovations produce culture and cultural analysis that do much more than reject the logic of an ocular and scribal European tradition. These opaque, and at times unintelligible, creative sonic acts sit outside of the accumulation of wealth, ideals of autonomy and the bourgeoisie orientations of ideal 'Man' and instead, amplify the hybrid workings of the human, via multisensory approaches. To remix Sylvia Wynter's work means to extend the notion of Homo narrans to encompass the ways in which sonic subjectivities leverage analogue and digital technologies to expand conceptions of Black life beyond the dominant narrative of our contemporary moment.

In the next chapter, the focus turns towards the turntable and the practice of turntablism as a sonic innovation. Across the various continents and contexts in which Afrosonic innovations occur, there is a thread of continuity that requires further attention. The turntable, made central to hip-hop and various other popular musics and examined through the lens of a technology revamped from commodity to instrument by Afrosonic innovations, presents us with an interesting coordinate from which to explore sonic practices of reinvented humanness.

2

Turning the Tables

'Things ain't the same for gangsters, but I'm too famous to kill these prankstas', begins DJ Dopey's word phrasing routine at the 2003 DMC World DJ Championships. Sampling a Dr. Dre produced Jay-Z record, the young Filipino Canadian heightened the anticipation of his six-minute turntable battle routine. DJ Dopey continues to build his stage presence, using a crossfader and mixer to cut in and out of two vinyl records, demonstrating the essence of DJ battles, two records, a mixer and imagination. 'When these beats bang, it'll drive you insane', DJ Dopey ventriloquizes his message, continuing a legacy of lyrical warfare that has its roots in the Jamaican dancehall (Cooper 2004). Various other phrases selected from Dr. Dre's rhymes, such as 'the best to emerge, the world is mine' and the song's chorus, 'I see you watching me ...', provide further context for Dopey's decidedly boisterous stage persona. This winning routine, like most successful turntablists' routines, is steeped in the legacy of call and response with its audience, but only if the turntables are made to call in a manner considered creative within hip-hop culture.

Turntablism is an extension of hip-hop DJ culture; it involves dramatically altering the sonic properties of a vinyl record using a mixer and two turntables. Emerging in the middle of the 1980s, Turntablists, stimulated by both Grandmaster Flash's 'Adventures on the Wheels of Steel' in 1982 and Herbie Hancock's Grammy award-winning 1984 track 'Rockit' featuring the scratching of Grandmaster D.ST (later known as DXT), began experimenting with scratching in ways that departed from the actual playing of a song. The Turntablist diverges from the DJ by refusing to play records in the linear and 'commonsense' manner they were designed for – that is, from needle to record, and from the beginning of a record to its end. An early commentary on DJ scratching is descriptively astute, claiming 'the scratch explodes all previous relationships to sound by completely repurposing the turntable' (Goldberg cited in Muede 2004). Turntablists select specific portions of a record and play this sound like a musician in a band: they use records as instruments and musical notes. Their interests are not in playing the song recorded on the vinyl, rather Turntablists create new music, eradicating an already established familiarity of the prerecorded sounds. In fact, many Turntablists perform together similar to a band, where each person is responsible for playing a specific instrument (Katz 2010; Smith 2016). The only difference is that these instruments are inventing notes from prerecorded vinyl records.

In DJ Dopey's winning 2003 routine, he decides to take a horn sample from a big band record and play this horn, rhythmically rubbing both the vinyl and the turntable platform in separate iterations to achieve the desired sound. Turntablism diverges from the sampling patterns of hip-hop music creation by actively manipulating a specific sound in a variety of ways with the Turntablist's hands (and sometimes other body parts!). Turntablists engage in various techniques to manipulate records such as word phrasing, mentioned earlier, as well as scratching, crabs and beat juggling to name a few (Katz 2012).[1] In his winning routine, DJ Dopey exceeded these conventions by first removing one record from the turntable and then tapping the stylus on the turntable's metal platform at rhythmic intervals to create a new beat; Dopey uses one hand to move between pushing the metal platform at his desired speed and cutting the sound of the record in and out of audibility using the mixer's crossfader. He manually masters the velocity, tempo and audio sample in a rhythmically percussive fashion. The needle, as it is tapped against the metal platform of the turntable, exceeds its initial functionality and is transformed into a drum stick to fashion a percussive instrument out of a turntable. Dopey's winning routine, easily considered an exemplary engagement with hip-hop's musical culture, was both informed and made possible by much earlier sonic innovations tested and refined by Jamaican sound system culture.

In this chapter, I turn to various performances and techniques of Turntablists to help think through the commodity/human/technology relation at the heart of sonic Afro-modernity. Attention is focused here on three distinct and award-winning Turntablist routines to help outline how sonic innovations operate within contemporary consumer culture, outside of the music industry yet

---

[1] The crab scratch is a technique that involves moving one's fingers across the crossfader in a slow motion to allow sound in and out of the fader while the opposite hand scratches the vinyl recording. The Turntablist's fingers resemble the movement of the legs of crab extending outward from its shell. Beat juggling is a technique that uses two of the same record rotating at different parts of the track while the fader cuts between each turntable deck emitting only a portion of each record.

adjacent to it. Turntablist activities are related back to aspects of Afrodiasporic orality and oral aesthetics, recognizing the historical embeddedness of experiments with sound. The final section of this chapter focuses on Rastafari linguistic practices and how they operate as a template of relationality, elaborating on how we might want to think about the role oral culture can continue to play in designing Sonic innovations and liveable Black life.

Beyond the DJ, who is the Turntablist?

Turntablism is inextricably linked to the art of the DJ. In defining the modern-day Turntablist, DJ Babu of the legendary Beat Junkies crew developed the first known definition as 'a person who uses the turntables not to play music but to manipulate sounds and create music' (DJ Babu 1996 cited in Katz 2010: 126). Although DJ is an acronym for disc jockey, in today's hypermediated and technologically saturated 'globalized' present, the function of the disc jockey has changed significantly. At one time, on commercial radio, the disc jockey solely introduced new records to an audience, which they could not see, and performed different forms of entertainment between the records and commercials. Many of the most popular Afro-American traditional commercial radio disc jockeys, such as Daddy-O Daylie or Dr. Hepcat, were steeped in African American vernacular practices that paved the way for today's hip-hop emcees (Toop 2000). Routed through Jamaican sound systems, Emcees and DeeJays emerged from the influence of these radio personalities – riffing on the chatty disc jockeys from New Orleans, Memphis and Miami who dominated much of the airwaves in Jamaica prior to independence (Bradley 2000; Barrow and Dalton 2004).

In certain musical genres, DJing involves more than the playing of records or being the 'soul controller' of dancing patrons. Within hip-hop culture, various techniques, such as transforming, scratching and beat juggling, have redesigned the interaction between DJ and machine technology, as DJ Dopey aptly demonstrated at the opening of this chapter. These techniques have increased the ways DJs manipulate vinyl recordings, borrowing from and extending how orality and technology intersect. Instead of a 'hands-off' reverence for the sounds recorded on vinyl, DJs and Turntablists enter into the project of sound making by using their hands (and voices at times) to interrupt the narrative structure and linearity of a record to tell a different kind of story. These stories vary with the DJ; they are both stylistic engagements with hip-hop culture and engagements that defy the already determined discursive structure of entity/sound engagement. These inventive new modes of existing with technology encounter the world through sound and often refuse the terms under which the dominant culture imagines itself.

The most well-known facet of the hip-hop DJ's repertoire is the scratch. Developed by Grandwizard Theodore in 1977, this fifteen-year-old aspiring DJ accidentally rubbed the turntable's needle over the surface of the vinyl recording (Benedictus and Frederiske 2002). He was simply following his Mother's orders to turn down the music in his bedroom when his haste caused the needle to produce a new noise once in 'illegitimate' contact with the vinyl. Before (and even after) Theodore's hasty blunder, the touching of a record was considered extremely taboo, a requirement of only placing and removing the record from the platter. Theodore's error was unknowingly the foundation of a new sound, the scratch, which grew to form the basis of numerous other techniques. Today, scratching is understood as a rhythmic manipulation of a record whose sound is sometimes chopped in and out by the crossfader of a mixer (Benedictus and Frederiske 2002).

The turntable has traditionally been a device that played vinyl or acetate recordings. It has a tone arm and needle that descend upon the acetate or vinyl and makes aurally legible the sonic matter of humans and their environment. The phonograph, the ancestor of the turntable, originally made possible the separation of the human from its sonic creations. Edison's original Tin Foil Phonograph from 1877 had initially been envisioned for a number of uses, ranging from letter writing and the teaching of elocution to the recording of family sayings and the last words of the dying. In the very family-oriented usage detailed by Edison in the June 1878 issue of *North American Review*, I am struck by his attention to the fragilities of human life, offering up a way to think about sound technologies in familial rather than commercial terms (Koenigsburg 1969). In contrast to contemporary imagining of the turntable, as niche fetish and as a purely consumer item, it seems the potentialities of the phonograph were imagined within the realm of the familiar and intimately connected to the delicateness and mortality of human life.

Early experimenters such as John Cage pushed the turntable beyond its intended function, rearranging its supposed use value. Like the multiple possibilities envisioned by Edison for the phonograph, Cage exceeds the assumed function and form of the sonic, pre-dating the modern Turntablist in this realm of experimentation. The presence of and desire to work with rhythm is one major distinguishing factor that separates Cage's experiments from what Turntablists do with turntables. Canadian Turntablist and DMC World Champion DJ A-Trak clarifies Babu's definition further, claiming DJs are entertainers while Turntablists are musicians (Webber 2003). While A-Trak draws a clear line in the sand, music as entertainment is a reality, but one he seems to neglect in the attempt to establish this avant-garde art form. In 1998, the National College Radio Association submitted a formal definition of turntablism to the Canadian Radio and Technology Commission (CRTC). Accordingly, turntablism can be defined as:

> Manipulation of previously recorded track(s) to the extent that they are substantially altered from their original format, and that the continuous or consistent alteration of the previously existing track(s) continues for one minute or more.

Clearly, the definition offered by the CRTC, a federal body responsible for much of the creative industries in Canada, leans towards a more technical offering and does not invest itself in an artist/entertainer dichotomy. This useful technical definition allows us to see how intimately the artistic practice is tied to the media industries and the role of intellectual property rights in controlling content. The kinds of violations of copyright Turntablists enact in their music-making techniques suggest their actions are both political and have an entertainment function as the audiences at the DMC World competitions attest. Turntablism inhibits a neat and clear demarcation of the often dichotomous representations of entertainment and art, consumption and production and Western art music and popular culture.

The Turntablist excavates various sounds and arranges them in a new sonic order that relies as much on a rhythmic pattern or reordered sounds as on audience response, which must confirm the legibility of this new creation. The call and response feature of Afrodiasporic life is central in the confirmation of a Turntablist's creation: in live settings, heads and hands must move in rhythmic unison, responding to the call and its creative manifestations. In performances, this interactivity takes places in real time as the Turntablist accomplishes a technique, the relationality of this moment makes legible these sonic innovations. When audience members catch the rhythm and use their bodies to respond, via head nodding, hands in the air or vocally adding to the soundscape, a Turntablist's composition is confirmed as a legible artistic creation.

The proliferation of Turntablists as band members, especially outside of the hip-hop genre, testify to A-Trak's distinction between DJs and Turntablists (see bands Sugar Ray and Beck, and pop star Nelly Furtado).[2] While Turntablists have made inroads into mainstream music scenes, just like DJ culture, turntablism mirrors the rest of the male-dominated music scenes. Well-known Turntablists such as Montreal's Killa Jewel and New York's Kuttin' Kandi stand out, with Kuttin' Kandi foregrounding female collaboration in her work and centring a feminist body politic in her artistic practice (Hisama 2014). As a music-making form, turntablism calls into question the relationship between human and sound technology by reformatting the use value of the turntable and recorded vinyl. Starting with fifteen-year-old Theodore and extended by Grandmaster Flash, DJ techniques annihilate a submissive reverence to machines and the assumed separation between human and machine. The irreverence for a consumer item, particularly through the very hands-on reformatting of the vinyl record, push us to consider how some Afrosonic innovations intervene on the commodification of music refusing the proposed (and commercially profitable) usage of vinyl records. Just as the call and response of Afrodiasporic life changed the relationship between performer and audience, the Turntablist and DJ move between performing for an audience, enjoyment with the audience and the total destruction of the invisible barrier between record and individual. These forms of relations, for an audience, with an audience and oscillations between performer and audience, speak to the sonic subjectivities articulated by turntablism.

Before 'turntablist' became a usable word, hip-hop DJs were experimenting with various techniques after the introduction of scratching. Most of the techniques that today form the backbone of turntablism, such as cutting or transforming, were practised by hip-hop DJs in vigorous competition, such as the DMCs, to see who could develop the freshest style. The earliest, most celebrated and best visually documented example was Grandmaster Flash's 'Adventures on the Wheels of Steel', an apt aural and visual beginning of what has become known as turntablism (Katz 2010). Using two turntables and a mixer, Grandmaster Flash played the instrumental of 'Good Times' while interspersing different sound bites/samples that explicitly acknowledged his DJing prowess. Flash's seven minute and eighteen second composition sampled ten different tracks, including Blondie's 'Rapture', Queen's 'Another One Bites the Dust' and

---

[2] Note how my examples are not only of Afrodiasporic artists, further demonstrating the wide applicability of Afrosonic innovations and their abilities to act as templates for new modes of human behaviour disconnected from racial schemas. There is also something to be said about the continued appropriation of Black cultural production in service of a wider American popular culture despite the continued dehumanization of Black life in the North American context.

the b-boy anthem 'Apache' by the Incredible Bongo Band. Turntablism became the heading by which the inventive techniques of the hip-hop DJ were nurtured into an entirely new avant-garde aspect of hip-hop culture.

At the core of turntablism is what some might call an 'unorthodox' use of the turntable and its components, such as the needle and tone arm. Such unorthodoxy appears only as such through modernist lenses, where authority and detachment dictate 'correct usage'. For example, instead of using the turntable's needle to extract sound from the vinyl, some Turntablists, such as Canada's DJ Dopey, refashion the needle into a sort of drumstick, tapping it against the turntable platter to achieve a new sound. Another way to understand the actions of the Turntablist is as an attempt at fostering a communal participatory sentiment, which subsumes the individual into the community. On a macro level, antiphony and call-and-response techniques are transcribed into a technologically driven aural, rather than oral, sentiment uniting audience and performer, thus fostering a critical alternative public sphere (Gilroy 1993; Neal 1999). On a micro level, the Turntablist's 'records are deprived of the authority and reverential treatment appropriate to a fixed and artistic statement' (Gilroy 1987). The Turntablist transforms the function of vinyl in the processes of making coherent sound, all while cannibalizing the dominant order (Gilroy 1987). Not only is the authority of the dominant order made ambivalent but also the pleasurable aural creations suggest a certain kind of alterity, where the visual is not privileged over the sonic. In these moments of aural pleasure, audiences are treated to another social arrangement in which racial schemas do not dominate.

While it is surprising that turntablism so quickly became a global activity in the 1980s, the multitude of different ethnicities and races which have perfected the art form is not so surprising. The art form offers us a way of negotiating multiplicity and difference, the complete opposite of the colonial projects that genocidally shaped the 'new world'. In a sense, turntablism embodies a modality of living with difference and heterogeneity in ways that refute the kinds of forced homogeneity that marked colonial expansion and the pillaging of the North and South American continents. The Turntablist, while stimulating the audience's aural appreciation, also produces a multisensory form of creative labour that frees the body from the reproduction of the social order and that disrupts siloed thinking and paradigms of homogeneity. In this disruption, the primacy of race dissolves and the sonic is prioritized, producing new modes of living in a world designed to support and reproduce a racial hierarchy. The creative labour of the Turntablist operates beyond the role of the disc jockey as promotional tools in the recording industry. The creative destruction of music recorded onto physical commodities for sale initiates a paradigm of transforming exchange value into use value, a decommodifying of the record as a consumer item.

What is also interesting about turntablism is that it operates through a medium that is seemingly outmoded and no longer a serious part of consumer culture; the turntable is no longer viewed as modern in the sense that cassettes, compact discs, MP3s and smartphones have replaced the record as sonic medium of choice for your average consumer. The analogue turntable, like the ex-enslaved individual, is modernity's excess and is discarded in favour of new and more intense forms of capital accumulation and technological development, such as the seemingly annually revised and relaunched iPhone.

The music industry's disregard for vinyl with the popularization of the cassette is mirrored by the disregard for human life during the Middle Passage and the first two years of seasoning in which approximately 50 per cent of newly arrived Africans died; the disposability of Black life during enslavement is mirrored by the disposability of technology when new forms of extractive techniques are formed. The piles of e-waste we find in Ghana today are contemporary visualizations of what the bottom of the Atlantic might have looked like as practices of deadweight tonnage and hefty insurance policies calculated the profitability of Black deaths (McKittrick, 2015).

With the Technics 1200 as the industry standard for DJs throughout all of the 1980s, 1990s and early 2000s, DJs and Turntablists operate through a dissonance that refuses to reify conspicuous consumption of technologies, even while the cassette, compact disc, minidisc and memory key trap consumers in overconsumption.[3] This dissonance is productive as it signifies on the progressive linearity of Eurocentrism, a linearity that imagines a 'better' future. Turntablism creates multiple meanings, troubling both consumer culture's rigid consumer producer dichotomy and the highly calculated manufacturers' efforts of planned obsolescence. By manipulating records, Turntablists trouble the archives of knowledge production that guide our contemporary world. Instead of demonstrating an 'objective' detachment from and reverence for pre-existing musics, these musicians engage in call and response and participatory activities, building upon aesthetic and oral traditions from the African diaspora.

---

[3] The Technics 1200 is the industry standard turntable originally manufactured in 1978. It was announced in 2012 that the Technics 1200 would no longer be manufactured, signalling the end of a highly unusual 34-year production of a consumer product almost unchanged since its original design.

As a Black expressive cultural form, turntablism takes its cues from the cut 'n' mix notion that comes out of Jamaican sound systems. Selectors, through practices such as the wheelback, routinely violate the reverence and commodity fetishism of the vinyl record. They break all the 'rules' of how to engage vinyl records creating new forms of relationality with the musical object and audiences, but they also template ways Turntablists would imagine their artistic practice. These cues are based on the idea that no one owns sound, that making music involves bodily movement and that the orality that forms part of Black expressive cultures can be elaborated, reproduced or refracted through technology (Hebdige 1987). This does not mean only descendants of Africans can engage in turntablism, but rather in direct contrast to such essentialism, turntablism involves aesthetic values and sound-making innovations that can be integrated into other kinds of social realities. Therefore, DJ Dopey's routine, detailed at the opening of this chapter, debunks the kinds of essentialist claims that attempt to connect authenticity and Blackness. Because sound can be disembodied and separated from its creators, Black musics are precariously positioned, ripe for capitalist exploitation and appropriation, but also they are aptly situated as paradigmatic in terms of testing new terrains of meaning-making and knowledge production. A closer look at award-winning Turntablist performances provide more concrete glimpses of the paradigmatic ways in which their use of the turntable provides a means to understand Black life and its relation to sonic Afro-modernity. The DMC winning performances of DJ Cheese and DJ Cash Money from 1986 and 1988, respectively, embody and emphasize Afrodiasporic oral and musical aesthetics translated into adventures of sonic subjectivities on turntables.

No seats, other tables

In 1986 at the DMC World Championships, DJ Cheese's winning performance oozed with references to and extensions of Afrodiasporic oral and musical aesthetics. Unlike the customary setup of two turntables with a mixer between them, DJ Cheese opts for both decks situated beside one another and the mixer setup to his right side. He begins his performance by bringing back the words 'it's time' twice on each turntable, allowing for the phase to repeat four times (0:48). A minute into the routine, he cuts the fader completely to his left side to cut out the instrumental and allow for complete auditory focus on his scratching of audio sample 'Pump me up'. Cheese spends sixteen seconds demonstrating a multiplicity of ways to scratch this word sample, moving between heavy emphasis on pump, then allowing the record to advance to the word me, scratching emphatically on this word before moving onto the last word of the phrase, up. He demonstrates his mastery over each millisecond of the record, managing with his hands the velocity of the turning steel platter while simultaneously showing off his range of scratches. Timbre, harmony and melody in this performance are neglected with the routines placing special emphasis instead on rhythm, timing, physical control and, of course, the scratch. At 2:55 in his routine, DJ Cheese slows down his power scratching, cutting his speed almost in half and the record's velocity, then quickly increases his scratching speed to return the record to its original tempo.

Grabbing the word 'huh' on the next record, DJ Cheese moves his routine along again returning to repetition, quickly cueing the word 'huh' on both records and eliminating the scratching. He moves back and forth grabbing and releasing the vinyl's grooves where the sound 'huh' lay, returning to each turntable four times. Cheese demonstrates his dexterity moving quickly between both turntables to the left of his mixer and his tactile sensitivity in rewinding each record quickly without making the needle skip. Here, Cheese contrasts the force and weight of his scratching earlier in the routine with this rapidly rearranged relation to the record, speed and delicacy necessary for this deft demonstration of skill. After taking a pair of handcuffs out, DJ Cheese proceeds to put them on and continues rewinding each record and focusing on repeating the huh sound extracted from the vinyl. Rhythmically, Cheese utilizes several baby scratches using the downbeat and bassline of the record (5:40) interrupting the groove of the other record in perfect timing. At 5:18 in the routine, DJ Cheese returns the fader to the left channel, cutting out the instrumental to again refocus on his scratching. For the next forty seconds, he scratches three distinct beats using just one record as cheers erupt from the crowd. Alternating between doubling up on his drums before letting one snare out, tripling up on his drum and eliminating the snare and then double timing the snare with only one downbeat, Cheese successfully transforms the turntable into a percussive instrument. Here, a recursive logic evidences a sonic episteme invested in inventing new relationalities to transforming this analogue technology into an even older form of musical expression, the drum. The vinyl recording Cheese is using is now repurposed to solely demonstrate DJ Cheese's prowess, the record's exchange value is reduced to nil as this Turntablist makes apparent its use value as raw musical data. It is only near the end of his routine that he lets the introductory bars of Dougie Fresh & Slick Rick's 'The Show' play for ten seconds. In doing so, Cheese certifies to his audience he has completely decommodified and destroyed the familiarity of the record only to reinvent several other beats in a matter of seconds. It is the familiarity of the record to the audience that allow his technique to gather cachet, he makes the audience aware that his tool of sonic innovation, a vinyl record, is a consumer item available for purchase by anyone in the audience. DJ Cheese's decommodification of the record demonstrates his dexterity and DJ skills, a prowess that cannot be purchased. In making new music from prerecorded sounds and commercial vinyl, DJ Cheese instrumentalizes the turntable to demonstrate a relationality that posits other possibilities beyond passive consumer. The dominant form of engaging a vinyl record is eroded by DJ Cheese's routine.

Pre-dating Olly Wilson's scholarly observations on conceptual approaches to the Black music tradition by eight years, Cheese moves through Wilson's notion of 'rhythmic clash', incorporating the physical body into his tricks and dramatically contrasting timbre in his set (Wilson 1992). DJ Cheese's performance comes between four and five years after Grandmaster Flash's 'Adventures', and in the midst of a DJ competition which until that time had been primarily focused on the mixing of records. Cheese's heavy emphasis on scratching and his showmanship of performing in handcuffs opened the door to the global popularization of turntablism as he, a native of New Jersey, was performing on the world stage in the United Kingdom. DJ Cash Money in his 1988 DMC championship performance did not just walk through the door opened by DJ Cheese in 1986, he obliterated the door frame, ushering in a new epoch in turntablism.

DJ Cash Money in the 1988 DMC World Championship Finals takes the scratch a step further, building the transformer scratch into his routine. At 1:19 into his six-minute routine, he cues up L.L. Cool J's 'I'm Bad'. Focusing in on the song's intro, a police radio that is 'calling all cars', DJ Cash Money manually rewinds each record to repeat the intro of the song more than thirty times, incorporating four full body revolutions to rhythmically match the beginning sequence of the record; after his rotation he faces his audience just as the first stab of the beat begins. His repeating of the opening sounds of the track stall the progression of the track. Never does the record's entire song arrive, building anticipation for the defamiliarized version of this song that will be born of his DJing techniques. At 3:40, Cash Money moves on to use the transformer scratch on L.L. Cool J's lyrics, such as 'I don't care'. With the transformer scratch having only been invented in Philadelphia in the mid-1980s, this 1988 performance on a world stage might have been a rare moment in which audiences could see the transformer scratch in action. On the words 'Rock the Bells', Cash Money continues his transformer scratch, separating each word and deftly manipulating the timbre of the sound effect to end his routine.

In his winning routine, Cash Money performs a masterclass in repetition working with four separate word samples to continuously repeat specific words. In three of these four sections of the performance, Cash Money delights the audience with a variety of body tricks, using his elbow, foot, nose and stomach to control the crossfader as he demonstrates his skill at repetition. Isolating and repeating the phrase 'Get down' at 4:34, Cash Money repeats the sample twenty-seven times, producing a stuttering effect on the word 'down', scratching only the beginning part of the word rhythmically in time with the same record playing on the opposite turntable (4:46). At 4:05, DJ Cash Money decides to reverse the record backwards, then forwards and then backwards again, with the crossfader rapidly moving in and out of the song, producing a transforming sound effect. The crowd's ears are treated to the illegible sounds of a reversing record whose counterclockwise rotations obscure most sounds recorded on the vinyl. The crowd's rampant cheering is interspersed with the sound of a foghorn, confirming that the sound of reversing vinyl and the visual aesthetic provided by Cash Money are appreciated.

These performances, like most Turntablist performances, diverge sharply from the historical lineage of the disc jockey as a promoter of records and as a radio announcer. By envisioning their performances as musicians engaging in an artistic performance, Turntablists sever the relationship between record industry promotion and the disc jockey. Rather than supporting the existing recording industry, the creative labour of Turntablists presents other modalities of engaging with recorded music other than the linear model of producer to consumer. The inherent exploitative possibilities of labour time, as dictated by the recording industry, are interrupted to demonstrate how to live differently with prerecorded music – in a relation that diverges from established overconsumptive trajectories.

Turntablism: Turning the tables of thought?

Sonically, in these epochal performances, as the turntable is made into an instrument, defamiliarizing the song has been central to the inventiveness and pleasure of turntablism. Paul Gilroy has suggested that Black expressive cultural forms 'transform the relationship between the production and use of art, the everyday world, and the project of racial emancipation' (Gilroy 1993: 74). Where Gilroy is interested in advancing a project of the eradication of ethnic absolutism and reads Black expressive cultures accordingly, I am more interested in how sonic innovations articulate a sense of liberation and template modes of relationality. The DMC Turntablist performances detailed here are generative tools for extending metaphors and methods for crafting liberation on terms ideationally indebted to sonic experimentation. Turntablism's many signifying practices trouble, on multiple levels, how we might understand consumption, recursive time and the centrality of creative labour in both pleasure and ideation.

Turntablists, reconfigure vinyl's use value, bringing into existence a relation that exceeds 'rational' consumer, as the proposed exchange value of the vinyl is creatively destroyed and reworked. When DJ Cash Money utilizes two of the same vinyl recordings to repeat one word twenty-seven times, not only does the word's familiarity dissipate but also the artist and audience focus their understanding of the creative moment not on the rehearsal of known prerecorded lyrics, but rather on the rhythmic patterns of the repetition. The Turntablist's and audience's defamiliarization with the now radically transformed word is accompanied by a reorientation to the sonic matter beyond its properties and towards its rhythmic pattern, and they come to anticipate, and appreciate, the frequency of the repetitive actions.

The original meaning of the lyrics, 'get down', in the DJ Cash Money performance, is performing its definition. This frequent phrase heard in funk songs is made to represent the creative energies of a hip-hop generation that exceeds the dancing element originally conjured in the term's use on funk records. Cash Money makes these prerecorded lyrics more than tools for a record label's desires of capital accumulation; 'get down' becomes a verb that is more than about dancing, it is also about demonstrating a control of linear time, consumptive futures and the process of commodification of Black life. This verb is no longer under the control of the copyright owners of this particular record, DJ Cash Money defines all the properties of this phrase and his audience through their affective responses confirm the Turntablist's proposition to radically redesign our relationship to prerecorded sounds. Like DJ Dopey's word play with Dr. Dre's lyrics used to open this chapter, Cash Money transforms the prerecorded phrase into a verb defined and controlled by his rhythmic innovations. The commodified forms of Black music and life trapped in a vinyl recording are remade into usable redefined verbs and set up new ways to relate to the commodified versions of Black life.

Turntablists operate through a relationality demonstrating other ways to utilize a record within our current overconsumptive realities in the West. In claiming 'our present "objective" mode of truth is only true within the specific terms of our present culture's self-conception', Wynter makes possible a ground to begin critique our present reality (Rorty as cited in Wynter 2003). Within Western economies of overconsumption and overdevelopment, the use of a commodity as a tool of music-making disrupts the assumed docility of the masses and the linear and one-directional transactive relationship required of music audiences to fuel the recording industry's 'growth'. Further, it is the creative labour of Turntablists such as Dopey, Cash Money and Cheese that lead us (the audience's affective appreciation of the revised sonic landscape) to exit the one-directional transaction subjecthood fostered by capital. This creative labour brings new forms of relation to the oral and aesthetic priorities of Afrodiasporic life through the subversive and 'unorthodox' use of a turntable. It does not go unnoticed that the very record and songs Turntablists employ present a mixture of new and older music, breathe new life into scraps of sonic material often relegated by profit-making entities as 'old news' or as having largely exhausted their potential for profit.

Turntablism's use of the turntable cultivates a sonic subjective that narrates a form of human life discreetly designed around the hegemony of Homo oeconomicus. The narrative of liberation excavated via Turntablist performances here uncovers how Afrosonic innovations propose options for human life beyond the ideal formation legislated through European colonization. So just as the blues were an alternative space of critical discursive engagement and knowledge production (Neal 1999; Woods 2007), the turntable, and eventually turntablism, neatly bring together aspects of Black living that work in relation to existing ocular-centric schemas. In the narrative invented through acts of turntablism, the labouring body creatively subverts technology to employ oral and Afrological musical aesthetics to liberate us (audiences included!) from market time and the linear progressive narrative of Eurocentricism. The allure of Black cultural production continues to be its ability to undo the constraints and limits of property rights thinking and extractive colonial logic.

Turntablism's decommodifying turn

The techniques of Turntablists urge us to reimagine our relationship to the supposedly fixed and predetermined pillars of our current mode of existence, such as conspicuous consumption in the Western world. The record (vinyl, archival and legal) then symbolizes the stability and the supposed predeterminacy of our times, while the Turntablist is the rebellion within our present order, refusing to submit to the chronology, linearity and rigidity of words and sounds captured on the record, refusing further to submit to the kinds of manufactured obsolescence that characterize all of modern technology's 'successes' in the marketplace. Turntablists work largely outside of market time, performing for niche audiences, rendering the sonically illegible as a challenge to the dominance of the colonial thirst to overdetermine the possibilities of human life.

Turntable techniques decommodify the prerecorded music held on vinyl records, removing the dominance of an exchange value for the physical item, the vinyl record. In the hands of a Turntablist, techniques such as scratching and transforming create value for audiences through emphasizing rhythm, percussive expression and repetition to the neglect of the song's carefully filtered design for commercial appeal. If we return to DJ Cash Money's performance, it is clear that repetition becomes one technique by which the exchange value of the music on his records is nullified. As the opening sounds of L.L. Cool J's 'I'm Bad', the sound of sirens and a police radio are repeated by DJ Cash Money thirty times, familiarity repeated consistently defamiliarizes as the context of not playing a significant portion of the song restructures the audience's anticipation. Rather than expecting L.L. Cool J's song to begin, audiences are attentive to a new sound or technique that will come next, but their anticipation is tempered by the repetitive notion of bringing back the record. The bringing back of the beginning of the song signals to the audience the musical form pressed into a commodity – L.L. Cool J's song – is no longer simply a consumable commodity, it is an open-ended formerly structured sonic entity that can foster innumerable possibilities. Turntablism turns these possibilities into compositional tools, proposing a praxis of being human that is more than over-consumptive 'Man'.

The Turntablist's composition, ill-suited to be categorized as music, destroys the established possibilities of the musical commodity and instead proposes a creative and active relationship with prerecorded sounds. The humanity proposed here is a relational one, one that does not solely consume from a passive position, but rather an active seeking out of connections, reconnections and other dispositions beyond Homo oeconomicus (McKittrick and Wynter 2015). The human, in the formulation proposed by the Turntablist then is one in which exchange value is a malleable suggestion that does not overdetermine use value. Put another way, the record label's proposed exchange value of the vinyl they manufacture cannot contain the imaginative formulations of activities fostered by a sonic subjectivity and demonstrated through a range of techniques.

In utilizing repetition as a compositional strategy, turntablism interrupts Western myths of progress. For the songs utilized in Turntablists' performances, the sampling of bits and pieces of each song deny listeners an opportunity to consume each song in its totality. The choruses and hooks developed in popular music, designed to allure consumers, as well as the intimately crafted, intricate and artistic chord progressions, harmonies and vocal range are completely disregarded in turntablism. All notions of time no longer belong to a formula crafted by record companies for radio airplay, instead time is accosted by the turntablist performance, such that its extension or truncation is defined by the artist in direct relation to the pleasure of the audience.

In the management of time, Turntablists can and do refuse the industry-driven logics of 'airplay', the standard popular song structure and the reproduction of a linear progressive narrative at the core of how Western Europe imagines itself and its colonial mission. When under the control of the Turntablist, the physical limits of recorded vinyl and its restricted sonic capacity are overcome. Duplicate copies of each vinyl recording are used to accomplish many techniques, and numerous records are utilized for one six-minute battle routine. The limits of the commodify form are exceeded, gesturing towards the limits of Western time as not an overdetermining factor for those deemed commodities under European colonialism. Here the Turntablists' 'disobedient methodologies' provide paradigmatic possibilities for thinking otherwise than of a rigid human as consumer, which is dominant in the formulations of our contemporary moment, namely Wynter's Man2.

Just like the remix, chronology and genre are thrown out the window, as are all other boundaries, in search of a rhythmic aural pleasure that sutures its constitutive elements. As a controller of the tactile, frequential, compositional and auditory elements of records, Turntablists enact a multifaceted deconstruction of sound, time and organization (Van Veen 2002). Through the eyes of the Turntablist, difference becomes compositional possibility, not that which should be shunned, segregated or eliminated, which is in direct opposition to how social difference is treated in Western liberal democracies (Lorde 1984). By regularly exceeding the presumed function of the turntable, Turntablists extend a creative ethos of liberation that re-enacts, outside of the enslaved African body, the insurrectionary knowledge of sonic subjectivities to exceed form and function. In refusing the West's discrete classificatory system and its associated silos, Turntablists elaborate a relationality whose connective desires bring creative labour to bear on the extension of orality and Afrodiasporic musical aesthetics to breach the consumer/producer binary and overcome the limits of sonic technologies and manufacturer's consumptive desires.

There is precedent for the wildly creative techniques Turntablists invent and refine; these techniques exist within a family of related sound-making in(ter)-ventions within the African diaspora, such as Trinidad's steel pan and Saint Croix's quelbe, amongst others. This relationship consists of utilizing what has been refused or discarded, in essence working with the B-side of modernity and globalization, such as empty oil drums, outdated vinyl or old car mufflers to create new and exciting forms of music. Steel orchestras developed in Trinidad in the early 1900s amongst urban Afro-Trinidadian men (Van Koningsbruggen 1997; Dudley 2003) after Black Trinidadians took discarded oil drums and learned to beat different sections of the oil drum to produce melodies and perform classical works by Bach, Mozart and others. Prior to independence, the steel pan was considered a 'lower class nuisance', nothing more than noise made by the country's poor African populations (Van Koningsbruggen 1997). By 1962, the steel pan came to symbolize the defiant anti-colonial attitude of the Trinidadian masses under Prime Minister Eric Williams. Quelbe, also called Scratch Band, is a music native to Saint Croix consisting of the utilization of discarded household items such as cups, forks and spoons to produce music. In 2004, the Virgin Islands made quelbe its official music, bringing this rich practice into conversation with the country's tourism industry. When not completely commodified in the marketplace, sonic innovations have been co-opted by political forces, sometimes in the service of nation building as Trinidad, Brazil, Jamaica and Saint Croix demonstrate.[4] The co-optation of sonic innovations tells us something about their potency and potential to speak to, with and for the masses.

---

[4] In the cases of Brazil and Jamaica, not fully explored here, I am referring to President Getúlio Vargas's co-optation of Samba music in the 1930s as he promoted previously outlawed samba schools in his nation-building efforts. In the 1970s, to push his democratic socialism platform we see Prime Minister Michael Manley appropriate Rastafari symbolism and reggae music in Jamaica's nation-building project. Prime Minister Manley's campaign song, Delroy Wilson's 'Better Must Come', and his carrying of the 'rod of correction' in public settings were two very clear co-optation efforts.

The lower-class 'nuisances' and 'noises' of the African diaspora speak the sound of their present, sonically rendering audible their status as human beyond object status. The repurposing of discarded items suggests modernity's excess, both in lives and materials items, can be imagined as more than disposable presenting a counter-narrative to extraction, consumption and disposability. Speaking the sound of the present involves subverting the discursive dominance of 'ideal Man' and its commitment to ownership and property as the guiding signpost of contemporary knowledge. But to think of the steel pan, quelbe and turntablism as avant-garde aspects of their times is to necessarily trap their genius within the confines of our present order, a space they have exceeded as evidenced by their very existence. As Kodwo Eshun reminds us, art forms are 'epistemological metaphors' (Eshun 1998), epistemes yet to come. The sonic episteme of which turntablism espouses gestures towards a multisensory and relational rendering of a decommodified humanity, a rendering completed through the careful and nuanced approach to liberating the labouring body using oral and aesthetic inventions (sometimes filtered through technology) and revamping the exchange value of sound such that a rearticulation of a more-than-'Man' human form might emerge.

To find Mozart in discarded oil tins in Trinidad, to forge Indigenous culture from the excess commodities of a successful Monroe Doctrine or to articulate other modernities in a (beyond) postmodernist fashion are all activities of a sonic Afro-modernity that is obscured but never silenced. Turntablism, in its noisy decommodifying tendencies allows us to rethink our present conceptual itineraries around culture, identity and technology. The act of deconstructing and recombining various components of sound to form new sonic arrangements is instructive in thinking about living with difference as compositional strategy in the design of liveable relations, presenting new rhythmic patterns of living that do not replicate hierarchical arrangements which dehumanize Africans.

The ideas that motivate such actions constitute recognition of the multiple possibilities for sound making beyond the prescribed role of the record player. Consider further the role of the body that both DJ Cheese and DJ Cash Money operationalize in their routines. Their bodies are in service of the music, not only responding to the call of the music and the response of the crowd but also physically embodying the timing, showmanship and dexterity necessary to create a sonic experience that departs from music but crafts a new narrative beyond the horizon of familiar songs. The use of the body, as body tricks, in a Turntablist performance is a reminder of the removal of the labouring body from productive market time. Body tricks, such as Cash Money's use of his nose to move the crossfader or the late DJ Roc Raida's over the shoulder crossfader technique, resonate with the role of the body in African musical sensibilities and aesthetics.

Like the toasting of the DeeJay in the Jamaican context, Turntablists enter into the structure of sound making as agents participating in the redesign of said structure. Turntablists refuse to separate meaning-making and the human, refusing to believe in the finality of prerecorded sound. Prerecorded sounds are liberated from their predetermined function, mirroring the process of the transformation of African labour from object to speaking subject. The dichotomy of entity and individual is shattered, forming new episodes of sound making whose 'legitimacy' does not belong to an Enlightenment inherited concept of the autonomous individual or state-defined freedom. Thinking through turntablism interrupts the modes of human life whose assignment of value is based on a highly racialized and dichotomous conception of European/Other, civilized/savage, with the latter always completely devalued as less than human.

A historical embeddedness of turntablism

It is tempting to imagine turntablism as unrelated to orality in the African diaspora, especially with its global impact and role of technology in making the artform possible. The turntable's manipulation and the taboo of excessively touching the vinyl recording comes directly out of the legacies of sonic innovations amongst Jamaican sound systems. The interplay between the toasting sound system DeeJay and the wheelback utilized by a Selector at the core of the sound system is nestled within generations of innovative oral inheritances – part of a counter-world of Black cultural production. Zooming out to recognize the social world within which the sound system was birthed and thrives, the dominance of oral culture in Jamaica is a significant factor we cannot ignore. From the popularization of the island's nation language by the poet and performer Miss Lou beginning in the late 1940s to the range of unique Rastafari speech patterns from the 1930s onwards, sound systems emerged with these oral influences circulating around them in their lived soundscapes.

Turning to the speech patterns of Rastafari, as linguistic innovation, they provide insights into the uniqueness of the sonic and oral Jamaican context in which we might imagine turntablism to have creative lineage.[5] Rastafari, a faith-based system born out of Jamaica's economic woes in the 1920s and 1930s, is an important site where the counter-narrative 'invents and structures its own symbolic order', which counters the dominant order (Wynter 1977: 22). Rastafari is the belief in the divinity of Haile Selassie as the descendant of King Solomon. Worship, dress, diet, familial lifestyle and speech are all dictated by the tenets of Rastafari.[6] Scholars suggest 'Rastafarians have done to colonial symbols what the Enlightenment is reputed to have done to tradition, authority and faith' (McFarlane 1998). Working closely with colonial symbols, Rastafari practices templated a way to rethink, revise and re-present information and ideas from a viewpoint that centred Black life and that was interested in Black well-being. They established that they 'knew who they are' in direct contrast to what colonial society wanted them to be – rejecting the idea of a white Jesus and embracing Garveyism's notion of Black is beautiful (Wynter 1977). For these counter-views and counter-narratives, Rastas were persecuted by colonial Jamaican society, regularly assaulted by police and forcibly had their symbols of strength – their dreadlocks – cut off. Another symbol of the Rastafari world view that could not be forcibly eradicated was their use of language, a usage that critiqued Jamaican patwa and embedded within it another world view of self in relation to one's creator.

Rastafari speech patterns negotiate a space somewhere beyond their colonially inherited English language and the daily use of patwa by the Jamaican masses. The use of the pronoun I replaces the 'mi' pronoun found in the Jamaican language. According to Velma Pollard's study of the language of Rastafari, the use of I is meant to eliminate the attachment to slavery and oppression that the use of 'mi' is connected to (Pollard 2000). Mi is considered a way to refer to oneself as an object because in Jamaican patwa me and mi are used as both subject and object (Edmonds 1998). The desire to refuse objecthood in Rastafari further underscores the long-standing cognitive autonomy that has been key to the survival of Africans through the Middle Passage. 'I-an-I' is an 'expression of the oneness between two (or more) persons and between the speaker and God'

---

[5] We know from the work of scholars such as Tim Lawrence that the splicing and editing of disco music also has a relationship to turntablism with extended remixes signalling the possibilities of manipulating an existing recording. The live editing and remixing of Walter Gibbons, Frankie Knuckles and Larry Levan in the American context can also be imagined as turntablist lineage.

[6] Haile Selassie is revered by the Rastafari, as a fulfilment of a prophecy by Universal Negro Improvement Association leader Marcus Garvey who told the Black world to look to the East as there will be a Black king crowned. He was crowned King of Kings in 1930.

(Edmonds 1998: 33). An interviewee of The Twelve Tribes of New York City explains the rationale behind I-an-I:

> We refer to one another [other Rastas] as 'I-an-I' – we don't make no one a second person. We just say 'I-an-I,' because every person is a first person. 'I- an-I refuse to comply with the shitstem'.
>
> (Hepner 1998: 211)

The oneness sought through the use of I-an-I is interested in refusing an ordered hierarchy so that 'every person is a first person' can mean a rejection of second-class citizenship or further social ordering practices that attempt to privilege one person over another. The multiple reasonings for the use of I point to the centrality of refusing object status in Rastafari thought, one of many thought systems in the Caribbean focused on the liberation of Afrodiasporic peoples. In this reinvented symbolic order, the African as object is rejected then orally reinscribed with another value system in which language draws a direct line to one's divinity. In this symbolic order, abolishing the familiarity and structure of any song, either in the dancehall as a participatory call-and-response scenario or in the studio in the case of dub music, is an extension of, not an aberration in, a counter-world of Black cultural production. An extension of the unfinished world of words and meaning slips into and structures both the possibilities of sonic innovations and the audiences' affective reactions and engagement.

In Rastafari, language is made relational to a Black cultural counter-world view, words are given use value and focus on rehumanizing the post-Middle Passage African. In what is also known as 'dread talk', the pronoun I is also used in the rearrangement of words such as vital, which becomes 'ital', and creator becomes 'Ireator'. The sounds of words are also changed to remove what is perceived as oppressive ideas in language. For example, within this counter-world of signification one does not refer to themselves as being able to understand but rather ovastand (as in the opposite of under) to eliminate the reference to being beneath a certain level of knowing connoted by *under*standing. Ovastanding is an indication of the desire of Rastafari culture to remove all oppressive mechanisms of language. These word-rearranging endeavours point to the importance of the oral and aural in constructing liveable conditions by Rastafari standards.

Rasta speech patterns create 'a new sense of self that leads to a new vision of values' that intertwines sound, power and a liberatory conception of the self (McFarlane 1998). I-an-I attacks chain-of-being ideologies that have suppressed

Black populations within Christianity and colonialism. The innovative phrase remaps the ideological coordinates of Afrodiasporic populations in the popular imagination, who traditionally have been at the bottom of these chain-of-being arguments, furthest away from a presumed white-skinned God. When I-an-I is used, it expresses an awareness of, on the part of the individual, a new and revamped relationship with their creator. I-an-I refuses the individualism of liberal Western thought and instead self-fashions a relationship with their creator. This self-fashioning is the explicit belief that one can participate in the definition of, and relationship to, their God. I-an-I as an oral/aural rearrangement expresses the ideal of participation in defining one's God and one's relationship to their creator. The manipulations of turntables, records and songs in the dance hall operate within this counter-world view and paradigm of creatively reinventing oneself (or song) and the counter-systems of meaning produced through such significations. The dancing audiences, those whose vocals call for a 'pull up' and those who sing along with a version, also operate within this counter-world of Black well-being in which symbols, language and activity are re-signified with new meaning, meaning that does not reproduce the harms of colonial violence. Participating in the creation of Black joy through an insistence on a multisensory experience of Black life is an investment in well-being (even on the dancefloor) related to the counter-narratives of Rasta language and symbols.

Importantly, a rearrangement of these words reveals how one particular aspect of Afrodiasporic orality expresses its rejection of European inheritance. I-an-I induces a subjecthood that encourages people to operate as active agents participating in the meaning-making of their social world rather than passive objects as was forcefully asserted under enslavement. These active agents attack present systems of meaning, exhibiting a willingness to engage with the meaning-making ability of words by intentionally signifyin' on words and their connotations. This level of creative labour, applied orally, transforms our relation to the dominant conceptions of oneself, a conception partially influenced by colonial discourses of racialization and hierarchy. I-an-I, as part of a sonic subjectivity, revamps both the meaning of certain words and our own passive relationships to the words we use. The rearrangement of lyrics, beats and sounds by Turntablists participate in a form of rearrangement through various techniques explored earlier in this chapter and extending the agency and utility of Afrodiasporic oral aesthetics – aesthetics that refute objecthood. Sound systems, emerging and experimenting within the oral counter actions of Rastas extended ideas of Black well-being and a willingness to take actions deemed necessary to secure this well-being, even if this meant misusing musical technology to achieve the desired results. The bold actions of violating the taboo of touching the record, wheeling back the record or talking over the song playing speak eloquently to the possibilities of violating social and colonial norms to the benefit of Black life.

In both Rasta speech patterns and turntablism, the written word and musical notation sit on the fringes of each culture respectively. It is through oral repetition in daily speech that dread talk mitigates the violence of the colonial project. It is the sound of a word that average folk meet daily on the streets in the highly oral cultures of the African diaspora. So Rasta sonic revisions directly transform the form and function of words and the sounds believed to be oppressive. These sonic rearrangements are democratized forms of liberation that operate through and are made possible by Rastafari creative innovations in sound. These innovations exercise a relationality with ideas and objects; they state a presence that interferes with the meaning-making potential of words inherited from enslavement and Eurocentrism. This level of relationality holds more meaning for individuals rather than the temporary disjuncture between systems of oppression, which is sometimes called emancipation. It is in this activity of interrupting the original meaning or exchange value of words that we see a connective tissue between aspects of a sonic episteme which assist in inventing and maintaining cognitive autonomy.

In the key of Black well-being

Within a counter-world of Afrodiasporic signifying systems, sonic innovations such as turntablism and dread talk encourage a renewed commitment to deciphering Black cultural strategies and the forms of human life they propose. If difference is the 'plurality of discourses, the perpetual slippage of meaning [and] the endless sliding of the signifier' (Hall and Du Gay 1996) thinking through Afrosonic innovations provides us with tools to navigate the multiplicity and versions of being human hinted at in our music, oral culture and sound practices. Both Turntablists and Rastas invent strategies and techniques to present us with multiple and relational possibilities for living differently. Securing well-being as a priority for living beyond the dominant codes of one's given society, either overconsumptive or deeply colonial (or likely both), the inventiveness of Turntablists and Rasta speech patterns present us with templates to live differently.

As meaning is always relational and connected to a system of absences and presences, and the work of the Turntablist is to make music from already recorded sounds, to create different versions from something believed to be a complete entity, then turntablism presents us with tools to destabilize our current regimes of thought. The winning DMC Turntablist performances detailed here highlight how 'African-derived aesthetics, social norms and standards and sensibilities are deeply embedded within the form even when it is being performed by individuals who are not themselves of African descent' (Schloss 2004). Turntablists, like the linguistic innovators of dread talk, demonstrate that meaning is not final and that participating within the structure of an entity, idea or language might lead to an idea of liberation unavailable through our current constructions of knowledge and social systems. The thought processes that inform turntablism, when lent to a wider project, like the conceptualization of the human, become viable alternatives in reconsidering the oppressive structures that dictate the lives of those racialized by Western societies.

When we conceive of a sonic episteme as an intentional structure of native knowledge, the pluralities that constitute African polyrhythmic sensibilities and the suite of practices Floyd captures under the heading of 'Call & Response', the human life forms brought into existence as a relational concept invented through sound are made conceivable. Turntablism and Rasta linguistic innovations embedded in dread talk form only a small portion of the numerous sonic and oral innovations that animate reinterpretations and reimaginings of a relational humanity as more-than-'Man'.

3

Riddim Science: On Living Hip-Hop's Sonic Innovations

Black music is not just another 'raw' material but one that comes with it, the weight and charge of subversive desire, of a subversive consciousness – one related to 'song' and 'dance'; to all that has no meaning, in the economic reality of the dominant order.

—Wynter (n.d.: 896)

Since ska's arrival in Britain with the Windrush generation, the reverberations of Jamaican sound system cultures continue their diasporic pathways as they find their ways beyond the island's geographic boundaries. Turntablism, remixing, dub and specific techniques such as the wheelback, beat juggling and scratching continue to make clear the more-than-'Man' articulations of sonic subjectivities. In multiple ways, in a variety of scenarios the unique perspective and aesthetic choices found in Afrodiasporic music continually rupture hallmarks of Western systems, such as linearity, progress, autonomy and the notion of individual property rights. A specific compositional strategy and musical aesthetic system emanating from sound systems, referred to by Peter Manuel and Wayne Marshall as the 'riddim system', has become a generative way to understand one aspect of Jamaican popular music. Defined as 'an autonomous accompaniment track, typically based on an ostinato', the riddim includes both percussion and melodic instrumentation (Manuel and Marshall 2006: 447). The riddim system involves the creation and circulation of instrumental rhythm tracks in a non-exclusive manner so that hundreds of versions of a song can exist with various artists singing tracks over them. The riddim system, then, embraces and organizes duplication, a multitude of differences and embodies an African musical sensibility around repetition (Henriques 2011). This sensibility stands in contrast to Western Europe's notion of art born from Enlightenment thinking. Riddims carry their own names, such as the famous Joy Ride, Pepperseed, Diwali or Flex riddim, providing an important way to index and archive this unique process of collaboration, use and reuse of these instrumental tracks.

Clearly connected to the legacies of versioning and dubplates, the riddim method does more than simply update and digitize Jamaica's musical legacy. The B-side craze of the 1970s in dub music, the euphoria-inducing 'specials' and dubplates owing to sound system innovations continue to be generative sites of musical innovation to the present day. Both in analogue and now in digital form, riddims travel alongside Jamaica's diaspora, finding resonance in New York, Toronto, London, San Juan and Panama City (at a bare minimum). With sound clashes going global, it is not unusual to find competitive sound systems from Germany and Japan, locations not known for their migrant Jamaican populations. In these cities and others, musical genres have formed and evolved operating with the riddim method as a significant factor in hip-hop, reggaeton and, more recently, soca. The applicability of the riddim system and riddim aesthetics across multiple diasporas, generations and musical genres warrants further attention as to the generative nature of this sonic innovation and DJing technique.

This chapter situates the riddim method as a sound system technique in which recycling, repetition and voicing are central features of its aesthetic. I begin by exploring the epistemological possibilities posed by the riddim method, thinking through the role of Afrological oral and musical aesthetics, technology and diaspora in this method's flourishing beyond Jamaican borders. Following this section, I examine the methods of living Black life through sonic subjectivities nourished and nurtured by sonic innovations in hip-hop culture, attempting to capture the fluid ways in which riddim aesthetics found a home within one of hip-hop's most creative inventions, the mixtape. I spend time exploring the mixtape scene that rose out of hip-hop in the Tri State Area but whose diasporicity located mixtapes in multiple global locations and developed local mixtape scenes far beyond the New York City. The final section of this chapter zeroes in on how mixtapes, lyrics and other hip-hop aesthetics invent value systems and a praxis that brings together oral and aural strategies combined with specific kinaesthetic practices to provide tools and technologies for Black living.

The riddim method as episteme

In the counter-narrative and counter-rhythms that Black musical cultures have expressed, there is a continuity we cannot help noticing. Call and response, polyrhythms, improvisation and repetition are features of various musical scenes across the African diaspora. The opacity of sonic innovations ensures an illegibility that allows the sound, the song or the technique to emerge even within a colonial government's oppressive regime. The intentional subversive use of technology, both in analogue and digital, is central to understanding how repetition, dissonance, voicing and remixing is achieved. It is useful to ponder the signifying gestures of the riddim method and the work of replication and repeating, of mixing, juggling and musical continuity in the narrativization of sonic subjectivities. The riddim method, as an aspect of a sonic episteme, provides a glimpse into Black musical experimentation beyond the aesthetic preference and logic of Western music making.

By embracing a process of replication, original lyrics and competition, riddims provide a bedrock for artistic innovation. When artists perform over a popular riddim, they are required to voice their songs in a unique manner to capture the attention of their audiences. The replication of each riddim with a unique voice allows for a repetition and extension of the sonic experience. Like turntablism's decommodifying tendencies and the abilities of dub to establish a template of decomposition and recomposition, the riddim method allows for a science of difference and repetition that refuses music industry hegemony. Manuel and Marshall, in analysing the coupling of voicing and riddims, note the acceptance of 'tonal incompatibilities' and a 'tolerance for dissonance' (2006: 460). Another way of scripting this feature of the riddim method is to return to Olly Wilson's notion of the heterogenous sound ideal observed in African American music in which timbral contrast is prevalent and celebrated. Wilson describes this dissonance, of vocal and polyrhythm in different timbres either shaped by a remix or a live performance, as illuminating the location of the music beyond the Western preference of harmony and tonality. When we keep in mind the historical context of open-air, outdoor dance halls, the economic imperative to maximize instrumentals and the traditions of toasting and improvisatory microphone mastery of artists such as I-Roy, Dennis Alcapone and U-Roy, and the features of the riddim method as always in conversation with participatory audiences, the musical aesthetics then align with the lived experiences in Afrosonic life.

In a dance hall or nightclub setting Selectors and DJs utilize the same riddim to create a seamless sonic experience extending the vibes for dancing patrons. In the act of 'juggling', Selectors will mix several songs on the same riddim, changing songs while maintaining the underlying riddim. While the tempo usually remains the same, the voices on each riddim often shift in tonality or timbre. Extended sets of juggling the same riddim sets up a dynamic in which notions of time and progress become entangled with the aural pleasures the audiences experience and the improvisational mixing techniques employed by DJs and Selectors. For example, some DJs have crafted entire mixtapes using only one riddim, as is the case with DJ Easy's pepperseed mix featuring twenty-seven different artists performing over Mad House Records' pepperseed riddim. Over fifty-three minutes, the mixtape provides a range of artistic engagements on the riddim, riffing off and extending the VP Records compilations from 2001 to 2010, which featured 142 riddims on more than one hundred releases on compact discs. The creative labour in which the continuity of a riddim is juggled structures an aural arena in which similarity (same riddim) and difference (of voice) coexist. This extension of time through the repetition of the same riddim refuses to replicate a progressive linear narrative of time, one thrust upon colonialized societies who were to 'evolve' and 'modernize'. The beginning and the end of a song as well as a sense of progression of a musical track then is consistently disrupted and controlled by the sound system's Selector.

The riddim method is not without its own politics, as it disrupts copyright regimes and the level of talent and creativity are deemed questionable by some. The riddim method is intimately concerned with audience, affect and participatory expressions, in a sense a way of evaluating well-being as a vibe. As a method, it privileges continuity, repetition and the relational connections to live audiences. It has sat outside of the 'economic reality of the dominant order' for decades, with a rarely enforced copyright regime in Jamaica and a different scale of late capitalist hegemony.[1] In dancehall music originally, but now in Soca fetes (in the diaspora at least) and in the hip-hop scene, the

---

[1] In 1913, Jamaica, as a colony of Britain, adopted the home country's 1911 Copyright Act. This law was designed to protect English creators, not Jamaicans, and thus was rarely enforced on the island. By 1993, Jamaica, now an independent country, had created its own Copyright Act. It is clear that the very laws of colonial society were never objective and the neglect of Jamaican creators in the protection of their creations appear aligned with a general othering of non-Europeans and a lack of equal consideration that mirrors in uncanny ways the colonial enterprise's racial hierarchy (in this 1913 law performed as nationality).

use of a riddim method now shapes and enhances the art of selecting/DJing. Within the Toronto DJ scene, it is not uncommon to have DJ packs circulated with extended edits – adding four or eight bars to the introduction – and during Toronto's International Carnival season in late July for tracks to be arranged in folders by the name of each soca riddim. This is an interesting migration of a tool that privileges audience enjoyment over copyright and property rights. With each different genre of music that takes up the riddim method comes the possibility of inducing or enhancing a sonic subjectivity beyond copyright logic, linear progressive time and the continued expressions of dissonance, improvisation and repetition found in Afrodiasporic oral and musical cultures.

It is in the art of selecting/DJing, in which the riddim method expresses its relation to a sonic episteme. In the Selector's juggling of riddims, the use of techniques like the wheelback, the impromptu remixes and the antiphonal quality of the continual call and response, in which the relation between sound system/DJ, record and mixing technique form a continual process of becoming (Henriques 2011). In this multisensory experience of the vibrations of sound cutting through the air, the physicality of responding hands in the air and the materiality of the dancefloor and speakers, human senses are not severed in the service of objectivity. Instead, an embodied knowledge of self emerges from the interconnected multisensory experience that refuses to solely privilege the visual.[2] Henriques suggests that this way of knowing as a sonic logos is useful in grasping the relationalities of a sonic subjectivity in which all 'knowledge' can be loosed, linear time can be severed and oral culture can be expressed through the manipulation of the records played by the Selector and DJ. Sonic innovations such as the riddim method gather multisensory tools to invent a rationality and subjectivity that makes Black life liveable as something more than 'Man's' Other or racialized non-being. These techniques and technologies for living have been captured nicely by the subversive use of the cassette in the development and circulation of yard tapes and mixtapes, first developed in the mid 1970s as party tapes.

---

[2] I use the term knowledge of self, borrowing from a hip-hop tradition, to connote the heightened social awareness of the ways in which one might avoid exploitation and dehumanization. In the late 1980s and early 1990s, 'knowledge of self' became a major theme in New York's hip-hop music closely aligned with a heightened sense of Black pride and symbolism (via clothing and music videos) that returned to aspects of the Black Power movement of the late 1960s. (See Gosa 2015 and Love 2018 for more on knowledge as an element of hip-hop culture.)

A method of rhythm: The mixtape in the diaspora

In recording live dancehall sessions, radio shows and other parties, cassettes became one avenue by which the DJ could continue, and eventually extend, the sonic innovations of sound systems. The mixtape recordings of parties by local New York DJs such as DJ Breakout, Brucie B and Grandmaster Flash would cost between $20 and $25 (equivalent to more than $160 in 2021) (Reid et al. 2003). These recorded cassettes played an early role in the dissemination of hip-hop music, with car culture also central to the popularity of mixtapes by DJ Screw in Houston in the 1990s. DJ Screw's chopped and screwed technique, a slowing down of records to a speed that distorted the voices of the emcees on the tracks, resonated with the desire of Texans to drive slowly in their prideful, metallic-painted rides.[3] Early on, mixtapes were circulated via taxi cabs in New York City, enmeshed in an innovative promotional partnership in which, we are told, that cabs, that some passengers used all day (hold cabs), played the most popular mixtapes on repeat (Shonberger 2010). While clearly engaged in marketplace relations early in their existence, mixtapes were not of the music industry in the 1970s and 1980s; as Thurston Moore makes clear, 'hip-hop mix tapes, sold on cardboard tables, began to head a value system dictated by whomever compiled the tracks' (cited in Shonberger 2010: 11). The mixtape held within it much of the DJ's technical prowess and their abilities to influence music culture with their song selection, remixes and exclusive tracks.

Within their early relation of exchange in the 1970s, the mixtape entered into local economies supporting young Black entrepreneurs and disseminated hip-hop music beyond state and national borders – their value system, Moore hinted at, did not solely align with the interest of profit-seeking record industry power brokers. Cassette recordings of local radio shows became one integral avenue in the circulation of Black musics in the diaspora as Caribbean migrants in various North American cities would often visit family members in New York each summer and it would not be uncommon for cassettes to be shared amongst the children. Such was the case with cities in Canada, for instance Winnipeg, Montreal and Toronto. Mixtapes, as they grew in popularity, did more than circulate the latest mixes by (mainly) New York City DJs (Odario Williams, personal communication, 2009).

---

[3] See the 2012 Houston hip-hop conference Awready (2012) for intimate details on Houston's car culture and the phenomenon of metallic paint. Also, check Houston native Paul Wall's verse on Kanye West's track 'Drive Slow'.

Mixtapes also allowed the skills of DJs to travel as well as the vernacular stylings of local emcees and mixtape hosts, spreading hip-hop music to places where the culture had not yet developed. Unique mixes of certain songs could travel beyond the borders of the United States, exposing DJs and other artists to different performance styles, mixes and remixes. Sonically, mixtapes captured and detailed a sonic Afro-modernity whose subversive technological adventures mixed oral, aural and kinaesthetic activities to disrupt Western musical logic and the progress of linear time.

As a promotional tool, mixtapes shared with the world the skills of a particular DJ and operated as a business card for potential party rocking services. Mixtapes, often comprising the promotional vinyl circulated to DJs by record labels (by the 1990s), connected multiple tracks and amplified both the A-side and the B-side of various records, creating and recreating an order of listening pleasure designed by DJs for the enjoyment of their audiences. New York's DJ Ron G had been one of the early innovators in this scene offering up a plethora of remixes on his tapes and establishing himself as a 'remix king', someone who took seriously the DJ's culture of mixing records and blending R & B a cappellas over hip-hop beats (Ball 2010). His legacy is cemented on the Ron G H & R remix of Mary J. Blige's wildly successful record 'Be Happy'.

Since at least the early 1990s, when DJ Kid Capri who was signed to a deal in 1991, record labels have utilized mixtapes and have signed and worked with many New York City DJs to place their promotional singles on the most influential mixtapes series. In the 1990s, the mixtape scene in New York City grew in scale, leading a number of DJs to up the ante to compete for the attention of consumers. Mixtapes rarely contained direct battles, instead it was DJ skills and the exclusivity of songs that distinguished some of the more notable cassettes which have gathered more attention via increased accessibility online decades later. For example, DJ Kid Capri's *52 Beats* mixtape featuring all classic instrumentals of songs sampled in various hip-hop tracks included no rhymes, just showcased his cutting and scratching skills. In contrast, the very popular DJ Clue produced mixtapes focused on exclusive tracks and offered listeners very little in the way of DJ skills, mixing or other techniques fans of hip-hop music have come to appreciate.[4] In some cases, multiple DJs contributed to the same

---

[4] DJ Clue's blatant disregard for the lineage of DJing skills and innovations has made him a target of other DJs, such as Kay Slay, who lament DJ Clue's prioritizing of exclusive records to a neglect of DJ culture. See Ball (2010) for more details.

cassette as was the case with the *5 Deadly Venoms* cassette featuring New York City DJs from five different boroughs. In many cases the mixtape's tracklisting and the DJ's transitions between each song formulated unique compositions and influential tastemaking abilities.

If we turn to the robust mixtape scene in Toronto in the late 1990s and early 2000s, one can find a surfeit of DJs and Soundcrews producing high-quality and highly sought-after mixtape series. The Toronto context, as a site that is beyond the national border of the United States, but also home to a huge Caribbean diaspora, exemplifies the impact of mixtapes as an entity with purchase beyond the New York context. As mentioned earlier, the mixtape scene in Houston, Texas, in the 1990s was also a robust site of activity with the circulation of hundreds of cassettes by the late DJ Screw alone.[5] Houston, in contrast to Toronto, did not have the same number of Caribbean migrants, so the DJs' audiences were less likely to be familiar with, or appreciative of, the sonic aesthetics associated with public music performances by DJs and sound systems. In the Toronto scene, two record deals emerged from this vibrant DJ mixtape ecosystem, Baby Blue Soundcrew's *Private Party* signed to Universal Records and DJ Mastermind's *Street Legal*, his fiftieth mixtape, released by Virgin Records. While these two mixtapes were signals of a healthy Toronto hip-hop music scene, I turn instead towards a mixtape that was neither organized nor approved by a major record label. This is not to claim DJs signed to record labels had no creative control, rather one cannot assess the creative constraints these DJs were placed under due to clearance rights and other industry concerns such as cover design, access to artists as well as production costs and timelines. As Jared Ball lays out, the inventive mixtapes from the early 1990s stand in contrast to the lack skills you find in the late 1990s with DJs more concerned with exclusive tracks resulting from industry A & R access. There is a clear trajectory in New York's mixtape scene moving from DJ and community creativity to a now 'industry-dominated medium'.[6] DJ Drama's Atlanta based 'Gangsta Grillz' mixtape series, which focused on individual artist mixtapes, and the 2003 raid on his home, which saw the confiscation of thousands of

---

[5] As of December 2019, during my visit to the storefront of Screwed Up Records in Houston, 341 cassettes have been recovered and are in the process of being digitized.
[6] Ball also calls DJ Ron G 'a true originator of the remix' (2010: 70). DJ Clue has been blamed by many for diluting the mixtape scene with his tapes lacking the kinds of creativity that is part of DJ culture, Oliver Wang gets into details, capturing DJ Kay Slay's disregard for DJ Clue. See Wang (2003).

compact discs by Federal agents (RIAA) and his arrest, speak directly to Jared Ball's claim of industry domination.[7]

While there has been a move to mixtapes as promotional items for individual artists, after 50 Cent co-opted the scene post 2001, I am intentional in remaining focused on mixtapes by DJs focused on sharing their skills and not simply using them as a tool for record industry promotion. An analysis of the award-winning *Reggae Meets Hip-Hop* series by the Soul Controllers in Toronto helps us grasp the influence of the riddim method in the Caribbean diaspora. In 2003, the Soul Controllers won a Justco Award for their mixtape *Reggae Meets Hip-Hop 8*, shining a light on a Canadian Soundcrew at this New York-based awards show for their innovative mixing abilities and remixes. In the local Toronto context, it had only been four years prior when the Toronto Police conducted a mixtape raid on 4 October 1999 (Wong 1999). The popularity of mixtapes in Toronto had become a problem for some members of the record industry as the quality of CD mixes began competing with record sales. The continued creation and circulation of unauthorized mixtapes after this moment provides some context around DJs' creativity, their networks beyond their local music scene and, most importantly, the continued demand by audiences. Toronto's mixtape raid bolsters our understanding of the potency of the demand for mixtapes and the changing technological landscape that allowed increased production quality that we are told could help them compete with officially released products.[8]

In a completely different direction than many mixtapes (including my own crew's, which often promoted new singles) the series *Reggae Meets Hip-Hop* distinguished itself by focusing on bending (mixing) and blurring the boundaries between hip-hop, rhythm and blues and reggae music. Immediately clear is the lack of relevance of industry-based music genres; the form of this sonic innovation demonstrates a clear divergence from the desires of labels to utilize mixtape DJs as promotional labourers. Each volume included a variety of instrumentals from all three genres, mixed with vocals from a different genre, so that dancehall reggae riddims were placed beneath the a cappella vocals of artists such as Beyoncé and Busta Rhymes.

---

[7] DJ Drama claims to have sold between 50,000 to 75,000 units of his mixtape a month, see Madden (2020).
[8] Kid Kut of Baby Blue Soundcrew shared this idea with the audience at the Toronto Public Library in February 2020 at an annual event called Before the 6ix.

Blending the instrumental and a cappellas, the Soul Controllers flipped the riddim method on its head. Instead of juggling many versions of one riddim, they juggle multiple a cappella vocals mixed into one or more instrumentals, sometimes looped and edited as a TV track.

Reggae Meets Hip-Hop 8 opens with its first track featuring reggae superstar Beenie Man's lyrics from 'Row Like a Boat' layered on top of Beyoncé's instrumental for 'Crazy in Love', which runs for approximately thirty seconds before a new instrumental is introduced. For the duration of Beenie Man's a cappella, seven different instrumentals are blended into the mix. In the diaspora, without direct access to the plethora of artists who might add their voice to a riddim in the Jamaican context, the digital copy of an a cappella is made to suffice. At 3:04, a Sean Paul dubplate transforms his global hit 'Get Busy' to big up each member of the Soul Controllers Soundcrew, continuing this decades old tradition and transitioning the mix into the next song. The compositional strategy of *Reggae Meets Hip-Hop 8* flips the riddim method, working with multiple instrumentals, promoting the DJ's mixing skills and song selection. The shortened length of each instrumental added to the mix, sometimes lasting a couple seconds, means the audience attunes itself more fully to the voice element of the song, anticipating the quickness with which the instrumental changes. The quick mixes of multiple instrumentals are built for the medium, as a prerecorded mix, void of a live audience, is designed to travel either via cassette, CD or MP3. By continuing to feature dubplates, wheelbacks and remixing, mixtapes extend and update the innovations of the sound system. Mixtapes exploited their medium while continuing to elaborate aspects of sound system culture in the Caribbean sonic diaspora. With the edition of an emcee named Jwyze in 2003, the Soul Controllers became more than a collection of DJs, but instead signalled their alignment with sound system aesthetics. Jwyze served as a DeeJay, adding vocal elements to tracks and transitions and eventually going on to have his own solo recording career.

One of the other features of the *Reggae Meets Hip-Hop* mixtape series was its historical timing, pre-dating the now industry standard digital vinyl systems, serato and scratch. The quickness of mixes, the precision of a cappella voicings and the timing of the entire mixtape composition was achieved beyond the merely analogue technologies available in 2002 and 2003. CD mixers were not widely popular with hip-hop DJs, so when a hip-hop DJ mixed a vocal into a track faster than could be cued using a stylus, it becomes clear a mixture of analogue and digital technologies are being leveraged.

In the continual transitions between reggae a cappella, hip-hop instrumentals and the unpredictable recombinations of songs emerges a diasporic sensibility that structures the possibilities of the mixtape as a sonic innovation. For the Soul Controllers in particular, but not exclusively, Caribbean culture creatively collides with American hip-hop. Via the mixtape, American hip-hop emcees are made to ride riddims and dancehall stars are made to toast over hip-hop instrumentals. The aesthetics of the riddim system and the techniques of juggling resonate in a diaspora space in which turntablism and DJ battles also deeply resonate with audiences and the generations of 'Caribbeans' already in Toronto, alongside a reggae sound clash scene that brings international sound systems, such as Mighty Crown, to Toronto from as far away as Japan. Not only was Toronto hosting DMC regional turntablist competitions but also the city was home to other local DJ battles such as the CHRY Metro Mix Offs, which became soft infrastructure for building a scene of world-class competitive DJ talent (Campbell 2020).

Not only is the hegemony of the author obscured by the DJ's creative uses of various a cappellas over different riddims but also the duplication and circulation of mixtapes made place and provenance important in accessing exclusives and regional styles of mixing and voicing. The voice of New York's Ron G, prominently smothering tracks, stood in stark contrast to Toronto's DJ Mastermind's mixtape series, which featured no talking on the first forty-nine cassettes. Despite being in a post-mixtape raid moment in 2003, *Reggae Meets Hip-Hop 8* continued to innovate with the riddim method, finding ways to remix this method in award-winning ways. The mixtape, masterfully exemplified in *Reggae Meets Hip-Hop 8*, comes to embody a diasporic sensibility in which movement and travel, nostalgia and remix, form continual strands of liveable Black life in which creolization, racial mixture and diaspora appear unavoidable. The mixtape is made to embrace and embody diasporic aesthetics that overlap with Black musical aesthetics so that sonic innovations, such as the riddim method, travel and augment along diasporic routes.

Toronto's riddim science

Audiences in Toronto have been accustomed to regular visits from reggae artists and American hip-hop artists dating back to the 1970s and 1980s respectively.

Other cities in Canada, such as Edmonton, Ottawa and Montreal, were also key sites for touring artists, but importantly Toronto boasted the largest Caribbean population and thus audience. By the middle of the 1980s, hip-hop acts from New York City were regularly performing in Toronto, often promoted and put on stage by local community radio DJ Ron Nelson. Toronto's proximity and substantial population of Caribbean youth provided the pull factors for emerging artists interested in testing new material. Attendance at hip-hop 'jams' and concerts were reported to have been in the low thousands due to the relative obscurity of hip-hop music prior to record distribution deals and the internet.[9] By 1986/7, Toronto's Afro-Caribbean youth were creating and performing their own version of New York's latest cultural invention; the Caribbean influence was prominent, exemplified best by a borrowed reggae bassline (from Wayne Smith's 'Under Mi Sleng Teng') in Rumble and Strong's 'Crazy Jam'. Signed to a label from London, England, recording tracks at Prince Jammy's studio in Jamaica, while living and distributing his records in Canada, Rumble exemplified the culture's hybridity and sound system culture's diasporic routes. By 1989, Jamaican-Canadian emcee Michie Mee and Afro-Guyanese emcee Maestro Fresh Wes became recognizable heavyweights in the industry, selling thousands of records and opening for major acts, such as Big Daddy Kane and MC Lyte.

As a diaspora space, Toronto contains a multiplicity of Caribbean migrants from mostly English-speaking countries, ranging in ethnic backgrounds and class affiliations. The mixture of social difference for Caribbean youth in the 1980s meant finding commonalities beyond their differing accents and non-accents. The hybrid significations of Rumble's recordings embedded within sound system culture as he rapped over the sleng teng riddim's bassline were not uncommon. Having cut a 7 inch record to test out his lead single 'Safe', on Prince Jammy's sound system, Rumble came to quickly embody and demonstrate the diasporic entanglements that would emerge in the earliest years of the Toronto hip-hop scene. More so than other early hip-hop scenes in Philadelphia and Montreal, the presence of Caribbean culture and its hybrid styling were more pronounced in Toronto, where thousands of Caribbean youth would attend all-ages events regularly. In fact, 'Jamaican Funk–Canadian style' the 1991 lead single by Toronto-based artist Michie Mee, featuring backup vocals by future

---

[9] See Ron Nelson's keynote talk at 'I Was There!', an event hosted in Toronto by Northside Hip Hop Archive, see RTAShowcase (2017). https://youtu.be/mZkXk27Wk2w

Grammy award-winning Jamaican dancehall artists Patra and Shabba Ranks, broke her into the American music industry after regularly dominating local competition in battles in the Toronto scene.

By the early 1990s, hip-hop heads in Toronto began rhyming about their city, signifying on the name, now rhymed as the 'Tee Dot Oh Dot', a simple vernacular intervention that pronounced and phonetized the city's abbreviation, 'T.O.'. Embedded in the city's emerging hip-hop sensibility, the 'Tee Dot Oh Dot' as linguistic innovation, relied on a phonetic engagement with sound to imagine and eventually perform another kind of Toronto. The remixology of a hip-hop generation's renaming of their city illuminates for us the operationalization of a sonic subjectivity in which Toronto's abbreviation can be re-voiced, versioned just like any voicing on a riddim. The strategy of re-sounding Toronto's abbreviation takes the accepted oral convention of abbreviating the city as open-ended, and raw material for a remix – no one owns sound. This phonetic oral innovation recentres Afro-Caribbean life in Toronto, installing a counter-poetics of being that forms the bedrock of another narrative of Black life in Toronto, aligned with a counter-world of Black popular cultural forms from Garveyism's global appeal through Rastafari to the present day.

Within diasporic public spheres, Afrosonic matter exists in relation to institutional power, legal regimes, community disagreements, race and class intersections, nostalgia and yearnings. The complexity of these spheres are expressed through various mediums and sites, from videos to radio shows, community newspapers and mixtapes (*Reggae Meets Hip Hop 8* being one such arena constantly negotiating vestiges of Afrosonic life). It is through the mixtape that a riddim science, an ethic which embraces the ideological underpinnings of the riddim method yet also successfully extends this form of radical relationality, can be created. A riddim science negotiates sameness and difference, rhythmically engaging ways of voicing difference in relation to an existing riddim. The *Reggae Meets Hip-Hop 8* mixtape is emblematic of Afro-Caribbean hybridity in Toronto's diaspora space demonstrating where the Black public sphere overlaps with diasporic spheres to mix, defy and refashion rigid notions of race, culture and genre. The mixtape, then, is a sonic argument against static renditions of cultural purity and retention, European notions of copyright and a technologically subversive extension of Afrodiasporic orality and musical aesthetics. The flipping of the riddim method continues to demonstrate ideas towards working with sound that refuse Eurocentric structures and thinking which close down (legislatively and discursively) the multiple possibilities

Afrosonic innovations propose. The oral and sonic inheritances of the sound system when in a diasporic context, mixed with the aesthetics of American hip-hop, produce the possibility of re-sounding Toronto and developing this oral intervention in a way that extends and remixes the Black oral and musical aesthetics amplified by the riddim method.

> You're tuned into T.O. creole at its best.
> Half of ya'll will never overstand the rest.
>
> (MarveL 1998)

These lyrics by MarveL, encoded within a counter-world of dread talk, demonstrate aspects of a diasporic consciousness of Toronto hip-hop artists engaged in Caribbean inflected speech and the ways in which Jamaican patwa both dominates and is inflected with localisms from the Toronto setting (see Elder 2016). A closer look at the role of vernacular innovations in Toronto hip-hop opens up the ground upon which Afrosonic innovations are imagined and negotiated. Caribbean Canadian artist Wio-K rhymes in his first single 'Sunlight' in 1996: 'without no Caribbean background, but still bussing slang that's Jamaican, but I'm not Jamaican / but at least I'm first generation, Canadien'. Here Wio-K highlights his use of Jamaican patwa despite his non-Jamaican heritage, demonstrating Jamaican patwa as a lingua franca amongst Caribbean diasporic youth in Toronto. In this rhyme, Wio-K invents a new relation to the dominance of Jamaican patwa in Toronto's Black popular culture. His francophone pronunciation of Canadian as Canadien locates him firmly within the Canadian nation space, where French is the second official language, suggesting his own awareness of his Black ethnic difference desires to disrupt the hegemony of the dominant language in Canada, moving from Jamaican patwa to borrowing a francophone rendition of self.

A voicemail recording from Wio-K's album *In Real Life*, released in 2008, perfectly captures the lexical and semantic transformation witnessed in Toronto Caribbean inflected vernacular innovations. Wio-K receives a message: 'Wio, what's gwanning man? It's me T.R.A.C.K.S. still'. The verb gwan, meaning to go in Jamaican patwa, becomes gwanning within the Toronto hip-hop scene. Gwan is a verb whose usage extends from Jamaica to Guyana to Saint Vincent, where its meaning changes according to the locale (Allsopp and Allsopp 2003). For example, in Saint Vincent, gwan can mean 'go and do', while in Guyana gwan can mean 'go away', or 'get out' (Allsopp and Allsopp 2003: 276). In Jamaica, gwan can refer to one's behaviour or performance, and in Belize, it is used as a verb for goin(g) (276). In the Toronto context, this verb is treated and transformed by standardized English by adding an 'ing'. Importantly, while gwan exists in Caribbean Creole dictionaries, gwanning is not a word that exists in print; it is at the very edge of our lexical possibilities – it exists solely in the oral/sonic. Situated at the edge of society's legibility, the transformation of gwan becomes a powerful symbol of mixture and hybridity that has successfully evaded commodification, dilution and eventual loss of significance.

Salikoko S. Mufwene's *The Ecology of Language Evolution* is useful in helping us make sense of gwanning. Mufwene explains:

> Linguistic change is inadvertent, a consequence of 'imperfect replication' in the interactions of individual speakers as they adopt their communicative strategies to one another or to new needs.
>
> (2001: 11)

It is important to recognize the historical embeddedness of this vernacular transformation that is taking place within the sonic environment of the 'Tee Dot Oh Dot', which makes possible its 'imperfect replication' written as T-Dot and, eventually contracted further, 'The Dot'.[10] Espousals of the term and its constant repetition (recorded on vinyl records) in performances, on tracks and via radio becomes a riddim, the cultural terrain upon which gwanning is a welcomed stylistic strategy in Black diasporic practices of identification. The innovation of this term is not about a return to some forgotten past, an imagined Caribbean, but more an example of the collisions of a 'chaos monde' (Glissant 1997) where the violence of the encounter produces new kinds of words and meanings. From this collision, Afrodiasporic populations produce versions and remixes – new and differentiated meanings and modes of conveying meaning, mirroring the process of versioning found in Jamaican sound system culture.

At this moment of treating this Jamaican verb as a standard English word, Afrodiasporic youth (and more) both decentre the dominant discourse that demands standard English and also transform the meaning of gwan. Gwanning sits at the intersection of Jamaican diasporic creole and standard Canadian English. Rutherford is instructive reminding us 'when the margin resists and discovers its own words, it not only decentres the dominant discourses

---

[10] Although beyond the scope of this work, there are likely several other terms that upon migration to the North take on new significance in a diasporic context – terms like lime, freeup and seen immediately come to mind. I utilize the Tee Dot spellling to gesture towards its phonetic roots recognizing that later iterations sought to write the term as T-Dot.

and identities that have suppressed it, but also transforms its own meaning' (Rutherford 1990: 23). Although gwanning is a decentring of standardized English, it does not necessarily decentre the hegemony of Jamaican patwa (Toronto edition), as one would have to have knowledge of the rules of Toronto's edition of Jamaican patwa to subvert these rules.[11] Nevertheless, it brings into relation a differentiated set of Caribbean (and more) youth in a non-hierarchical way that embraces, yet remixes, the Jamaican derived lingua franca. The circulation of terms such as gwanning occurs through radio programmes and locally produced records as well as, of course, at parties.

Gwanning, as the result of the collision of two systems of knowledge, reinvents and re-narrates Toronto as a 'home' for diasporic youth who are excluded by the dominant discourse and whose diasporic subjectivities cast them outside of 'authentic' Caribbean culture, especially by those directly from the region (Campbell 2012). This lexical invention/intervention, born in the Toronto context whose existence is firmly routed in the experience of being diasporic, operates as a sonic distortion that dubs gwan, refracting standardized English language in the Canadian context. The imperfect replication of the written form of the T-Dot, as captured on vinyl recordings, duplicates and transforms this lyrical intervention by circulating multiple versions, with the phonetic 'Tee Dot Oh Dot', sitting alongside the written T-Dot and the oral variations: 'Tee Dot', 'the Dot' and 'T.O.'. By being grounded in oral culture, gwanning resists materialization and becomes a temporal sonic innovation that reverberates a Caribbean sensibility throughout Toronto to tell a different story about being diasporic Caribbean. Like the word Tee Dot Oh Dot, gwanning, as an invention of Afrodiasporic Caribbean youth in Toronto, is an oral technology that opaquely operates as a site of identification that does the work of structuring a sense of belonging in Caribbean diasporic contexts. These invented terms provide a bedrock upon which specific behaviours – a praxis – can be developed to live in an anti-Black diaspora space.

The milieu in which the term gwanning is made possible is perhaps best exemplified by the track 'T-Dot Anthem' in 2001. Rather than being just an ode to the city, the track released by DJ T.R.A.C.K.S.'s crew, IRS,[12] is a complete

---

[11] The popularization of Jamaican patwa in the diasporic context of Jamaica, despite little formal studies or public discourse on the topic, means the intimate rules and nuances of how Jamaican nation language augments in the diasporic context of Toronto remain largely undertheorized. Terms fade in and out of usage and beyond the very recent work of scholars such as Clive Forrester: see Forrester (2007).

[12] Pronounced phonetically, this acroymn for Instinctive Reaction to Struggle distinguishes itself from the U.S. government authority yet draws on powerful conntations of the term. Thanks to Ellie Hisama for reflecting with me on this interesting dynamic.

revisioning of the Toronto city space in which young people take on Caribbean cultural traits. On this track, IRS claims they are from a city where 'we all rude', where you 'cannot find a girl without an attitude'. The city, according to IRS, is 'full of pure badman'. Initially, these assertions appear rather offensive, but read within the context of the Caribbean cultural residues, it is not as insulting as one might imagine. The Badman, born out of Jamaica's 1960s Rudebwoy and Trinidad's Badjohn subcultures is an affirmation of an unwillingness to be exploited within the clutches of Babylon's capitalist regime.[13] Similarly, to be rude or have an attitude is seen as a tool of self-fashioning to resist exploitation and oppression. Embedded in IRS's lyrics are clear affirmations of the counter-world and counter-narratives made possible by Black popular culture and music dating back to Marcus Garvey and the various symbols birthed from Rastafari culture. A rejection or refusal of the dominant codes, a praising of rudeness situates hip-hop music as one site by which diasporic articulations of Black life appears in multiple forms, tactically deployed and culturally celebrated.

A gendered reading of rudeness understands the female that is rude as a self-knowing woman of integrity, a quality that can demonstrate a sense of confidence and awareness. Lyrically, IRS actively engages in the use of Caribbean culture to meet their desire to make Toronto home, employing language as a 'diasporic resource' to develop alternative values and narratives that draw on Caribbean culture in nourishing ways (Brown 2009: 42). The resources deployed here are embedded in oral and sonic innovations, which re-voice notions of belonging and home against the rhythms of social exclusion in the Canadian nation space. The Caribbean vernacular found in 'T-Dot Anthem', besides sprinkling the track with flavourful lyricism, expresses one of the fundamental tactics by which 'otherized' Afro-Caribbean youth engage in identity politics: representin'. Outernational yearnings, both in a nostalgic fashion and a revised edition, become toolkits, diasporic resources by which counter-identities are posited and fashioned. For these youth, as both Canadian-born and part of the 1.5 generation,[14] the use of counter, encoded or opaque meaning-making strategies carve out spaces for identity negotiation rather than acceptance of state otherizing strategies. Such diasporic resources help circumvent the limits

---

[13] Rudeness in this scenario refracts the dominance of Westerns and American cowboy films on Jamaican television, with young men taking on John Wayne-like qualities in the streets of Kingston.
[14] The 1.5 generation consists of those who are born in their home country and migrate elsewhere during their formative years which are influenced by the new country.

of Toronto time and space, calling into question the local/present and inventing subjectivities routed through sonic innovations.

The space IRS seeks to represent cannot and does not rely solely on the discursive terrain of the nation state (McKittrick 2006). In fact, the title of their album, *Welcome to Planet IRS*, tells us much about their signifying practices in relation to physical space. The album's third release, 'T.R.A.C.K.S. Lament 1.5', a short and melodic track of under three minutes, diverges from the standard popular music track, with only one verse shared between two emcees and more than one minute of introductory instrumental music. The rhyming at 1:05 opens with Black Cat being explicitly clear when he rhymes not just utopian ideals but also their imagined origin story, 'we come from planet IRS where there's no prejudice or bigotry'. He is clearly not longing for an imagined return, but rather confidently asserting his identity and ethical roots, which apparently are dissimilar from his current society. Korrey Deez finishes the verse, 'this is a new way of thinking with new philosophies, making our hope of how it ought to be. We establish the better system where the people live properly, change the impossible to probably' (1:15). These lyrics hint at desires beyond representation, to a sort of structural change, something that exists beyond the nation state. The importance of the local in their album, on singles like 'T-Dot Anthem', is tempered by their otherworldly imagining, gesturing towards an Afrofuturst ideal without fully committing their project to the outer planetary yearnings of artists such as Sun Rah and George Clinton.

IRS's spatial refashioning of the host nation, through ingenious rhymes and multilayered metaphor usage, retrieves the appropriate tools for navigating the discursive terrain of a Toronto dominated by educational, judicial and political institutions modelled on anti-Blackness. The subjectivities proposed by IRS rely on vestiges of Afrosonic cultures to transcend national and imagined borders and achieve a goal that arguably is about securing a sense of belonging and comfort. Linguistic acrobatics and sonic ingenuity, extended from the innovations of DeeJays in sound system culture and American Disc Jockeys, are tools to make protectively opaque the necessary sonic weaponry to erect human forms that narrate a version of the human not Eurocentically overdetermined.

IRS represents in a fashion that does not mimic the posturing of commercially successful 'gangster' rap; visually, they refuse images of conspicuous consumption, the degradation of women and the plethora of guns one might see in early NWA or Ice-T videos. In fact, IRS explicitly rejects the popular rating system from the American hip-hop magazine *The Source* and their five mics system of rating albums, as Black Cat confidently asserts on 'T-Dot Anthem', 'we don't need five mics to call ourselves classic!' IRS boldly asserts a value system for their work that is not reliant on reproducing aspects of American media imperialism, which influence access to artists and inadvertently erect metrics of success scaled to a country of hundreds of millions in contrast to Canada's population of thirty-seven million. Members of the Toronto hip-hop community are shouted out, as IRS honours those that purchase and support their music, play their videos, spin their music and attend their shows. Thus, college community radio stations CIUT, my former station CHRY, and CKLN are part of the shout out. Recognition of the community that supports and nurtures IRS's art is a counter-hegemonic activity, a form of reppin' that stresses alternatives to the pathologizing discourses that paint hip-hop culture with the misogynistic brush of commercially-orientated rap music (Forman 2002). Unlike the images of gangster rap that proliferate on mainstream media, women are in large part absent from the video. The only woman in the video is a Circle crew member, Tara Chase, whose lyrical prowess rather than visual representation is how she gained critical acclaim from her hip-hop peers.

In the video, there is no distinction in performance between the men in the video and the lone woman, Chase – they all clamour for representational space in front of the camera. Chase's womanhood does not find a specific representational form; her gestures and body language replicate those of the men in the video, highlighting contemporary hip-hop's binarism in which female emcees are offered two problematically rigid subject positions – masculinist posturing or oversexualized and objectified eye candy. Chase's presence in the 'T-Dot Anthem' video, then, highlights how a hip-hop crew attempts to walk outside of the misogynistic rapper stereotype and the associated visuals.

The video for 'T-Dot Anthem' is a spatial exploration of IRS's identity politics, centring their activities at Toronto City Hall and outside an independently owned and operated late-night fast food joint, Johnny's Burgers, amongst other known city sites. For the majority of the video, emcees Black Cat and Korry Deez stand on stage at a podium in the courtyard of Toronto City Hall. As they reassure us of their crew's lyrical dopeness, IRS also outlines exactly how they will relay their ethnographic survey of *their* Toronto. Part imagination, part nostalgia, the cityscape renderings of 'T-Dot Anthem' are as important as those who relay the information. At the podium, IRS purposely inhabits a space imbued with power – the political and physical centre of the city. Black Cat, DJ T.R.A.C.K.S. and

Korry Deez, as Afro-Caribbean children of immigrants, centre themselves in the middle of Toronto and force their way into the discursive machinations of a city in which marginalized non-whites are too often silenced, criminalized or homogenized (Clarke 1997; Philip 1998; James 2001).

A reading of 'T-Dot Anthem' illuminates the use of Caribbean cultural tropes as diasporic tools to reinvent a different kind of base superstructure relationship. Products of the Toronto's education system (including the post-secondary system), IRS does not appear to reproduce the conditions of their emergence as 'otherized' non-Canadians. Instead of reinscribing themselves as marginal to the centre of Toronto and its politics, IRS posits another, more central relationship to society's institutions and ideologies. Notably, they lyrically and physically secure a discursive and literal centrality as non-marginalized, non-immigrant Canadians. Their embrace and utilization of the term the T-Dot makes possible a re-voicing of one's belonging to the city as the term's repetition and circulation form a discursive landscape – a riddim track upon which Black life can be imagined and reimagined beyond the dominant discourse. The version of Toronto outlined by IRS is a B-side, a muted narrative made inaudible by dominant A-side discourses that alienate Caribbean populations. In their formulation, just like the experimental remixes we might find on the B-side of a dub record, IRS provides us with a narrative of Afro-Caribbean life in Toronto that is not circulated through the numerous dominant communication vehicles, for instance commercial radio and mainstream newspapers. The B-side IRS provides us with is experimental, hybrid and filters out the vestiges of anti-Blackness in their local context and instead installs and amplifies a way to read and decipher what it means to live in Toronto as the children of Caribbean immigrants through a lens of the sonic. This track, like most of the tracks on their album, *Welcome to Planet IRS*, echoes sentiments of Caribbean oral cultures re-voicing their presence in the Toronto diaspora space to critique power and rearticulate another kind of relationality.

In combination with their detailed lyrical display, IRS, through the negotiations of space, produce another meaning, duplicated and circulated on radio, vinyl and CD, of how immigrant youth might relate to their city. By operating through the very tropes of otherness used against them by the state, IRS, with diasporic resources such as 'Badman', rudeness and the locally ingenious 'T-Dot', recycle and layer counter-narratives onto a new articulation of self, a subjectivity invested in other kinds of representations of Black life. IRS's oral and sonic aesthetics operate through an episteme that chooses to borrow, improvise and remix words, sounds and music in a radical relationality that might mitigate anti-Blackness. This mode of both reasoning and existing, reflecting the Turntablists' art and a cut 'n' mix attitude, evades a concrete reading by disciplinary hegemonic forces interested in taming and making culture static, like state-sponsored multiculturalism in Canada. Living life in the mix and continually participating in the development and redevelopment of meaning, allows IRS's art to speak with and to a generation whose diasporic routes root them in spatial-sonic temporalities that rely on Black musical aesthetics to construct subjectivities anchored by sonic innovations.

The 6ix

'Tee Dot Oh Dot', while emerging in the early 1990s, and through repetition and recorded duplication in hip-hop tracks and live performances (as the Tee Dot), established a sonic subjectivity for Toronto-based youth from the Caribbean diaspora. Today, alongside a demographic shift of less Caribbean migrants, we witness the emergence of a new nickname for the city of Toronto, the 6ix. The new term's emergence makes clear the extent to which younger generations, those born in the 1990s into the language of the Tee Dot, have accepted Toronto as a home for hip-hop culture by actively engaging in its newest nickname. The creative wordplay of this term operate as a new generation's voicing of belonging, another version made possible by and layered atop of the T-Dot riddim. Rapper Jimmy Prime's 2013 vernacular innovation, as author of the term the 6ix, is a prime example of how sonic subjectivities nurture new imaginings of relation. In his desire to rename the city, it appears Jimmy felt a sense of belonging to Toronto or at least believed his city, was a place he could represent in his hip-hop music. A renaming suggests a sense of attachment in the desire for a reattachment to the city space. When the phrase the Tee Dot Oh Dot was invented by K4ce in the early 1990s, his invention was about referencing *his* city in a way that aligned with his cultural immersion in hip-hop culture. In the late 1990s and early 2000s, as the term gathered traction with its use by the next generation of emcees, such as Saukrates, Monolith and Choclair, and as the term was duplicated on vinyl, it became more clear how the 'Tee Dot' functioned as a counter-narrative – rendering Toronto home for the purposes of creatively reimagining one's existence through rhymes rather than racial scripts. While some view the popularity of the 6ix as a 'global rebrand' and as the end of the nickname the T-Dot, I suggest a more connected and nuanced relationship between the two nicknames for Toronto (Lipscombe 2016).

Former *Degrassi Junior High* actor, turned international chart-topping rapper, Aubrey 'Drake' Graham's prolific use of the term the 6ix has helped it gain worldwide traction and transcend hip-hop audiences. In Toronto, radio stations that don't even play hip-hop or 'urban' music refer to Toronto as the 6ix. Additionally, CBC radio, Canada's crown corporation (similar to the BBC in the UK), also took up the new nickname, hosting a songwriting contest for new anthems for the 6ix, called 'Songs in the 6ix'. The acceptance of the term and its use, while not overly connected with an ethical acceptance or celebration of Blackness, demonstrate how Afrosonic innovations recalibrate public spheres, even if only symbolically, so that forms of belonging might develop even in the midst of anti-Black institutions such as the police and schools.

Today's transformation of the city from the Tee Dot Oh Dot to the 6ix is much more than a slick marketing campaign by the team at Drake's record and clothing company, OVO. A surface level reading of the ways in which Drake has attempted to popularize Toronto as the 6ix reads as yet another vernacular youth fad. Media outlets print frivolous articles that debate their own uses of the term the 6ix and their own editorial rules, a weird kind of navel gazing whose only function appears to simply align the publication with usage of the word the 6ix.[15] Longer and more engaged pieces such as Faziah's 'Hip Hop Before Drake' in *Fader* and Lipscombe's 'This is a 6 God Dream' (2016) and Lowers' 'Drake: King of the North' (2016), both in *Exclaim*, fail to draw links between the Tee Dot Oh Dot and the 6ix as forms of poiesis that recalibrate social relations. What these nicknames have accomplished is to redesign how publics imagine Toronto, and they do so with Afrosonic vernacular innovations as foundational to such discussions and relational imaginings. The redesign of publics, or the social transformation initiated by both the '6ix' and the 'Tee Dot Oh Dot' began almost three decades ago when the sound and the lyrical acrobatics of emcees, decided to re-voice a sense of belonging on the riddim of Toronto.

---

[15] See John McConnell's piece in the very conservative national newspaper, the *Globe and Mail* (McConnell 2015). See also Eric Andrew-Gee's piece in the same newspaper one year later (Andrew-Gee 2016).

Still though ...

Labour time is not man's lifetime. Man's vital demand is the demand to participate in the constitution of a sense of self-worth by and through his creative actions upon the world.

—Wynter (n.d.: 734)

Like the Turntablist whose hands-on mastery of different velocities, timbres, pitches and tempos (in microseconds!), sonic subjectivities work across a range of heterogenous musical and sonic formations to imagine and materialize another narrative of living beyond biocentric man. Sonically rendered constructions of home evident in Toronto hip-hop music present us with a concrete example of the material impacts of sonic subjectivities. The riddim method's use of repetition, combined with the duplication of mixtapes and their diasporic traversing of Caribbean soundscapes beyond the region demonstrate how the creative labour of sonic innovations directly contradict European musical sense, its copyright regime and recursively resignify Western linear time. The constitution of self, imagined and materialized through the sonic, emerged outside of market-time, carrying with it high residues of orality and Afrosonic innovation. Such tools, from dubplates, call and response and wheelbacks to remixes, continually deployed by DJs, sound systems and Deejays/Emcees inform a re-voiced riddim track of Black life amendable to remixing, versioning, imperfect replication and the invention of other kinds of relations.

When released from the overdetermining logics of racial schemas, sonic subjectivities can and do invent new relations, such that one's life in Toronto might be informed by a diasporic sensibility, urging a recalibration of one's socially engineered marginalization. In such a context, the creative labour and aesthetic investments of hip-hop culture routed themselves through sound, language and Black geographies, to remix and replicate another version of Toronto sonically rendered as an ethical site of belonging. The hip-hop mixtape, with its technological subversion, disrespect of copyright and embedded musical and oral aesthetics, captures perfectly and replicates the workings of sonic subjectivities that inform our behaviours within the visual regime of European thinking. At various calibrations and velocities, Afrosonic innovations provide methods and metaphors for the existence of forms of human life in its multisensory oral, aural, kinaesthetic and visual relationalities. Living within the relation invented by the Tee Dot Oh Dot, a B-side remixed version of Toronto loosens the forms of knowledge that underpin the racial logics of coloniality. The home that becomes audible on the B-side version of Toronto is one whose milieu, from the city's rich histories of sound systems to the independently circulated hip-hop vinyl of the 1990s, continuously extended and deployed Black music aesthetics and sonic innovations. In so doing, the sonic infrastructure invented by Selectors, Turntablists and DeeJays/DJs allows for another rhythm of living with heterogenous sound.

In the next chapter, my focus moves from the turntable to the mixing board and practices of remixing exemplified in remix culture and dub music. My interest lies in elaborating how dub and the remix express sonic subjectivities that negotiate, illuminate and extend the multiplicities of sonic tools, aesthetics and strategies embedded in sonic Afro-modernity.

4

Dubbing the Remix and Its Uses

Narrative originality lodges not in making up new stories, but in managing a particular interaction with this audience […] at every telling the story has to be introduced uniquely into a unique situation … formulas and themes are reshuffled rather than supplanted with new materials.

—Ong (1982: 42–43)

Polyrhythmic music provides a primary and unusually intuitive avenue, not just to conceptualize, but to train ourselves to cross and combine heterogeneous spaces, chaotic rupture, and zones of communication directly into our body-minds.

—Davis (2008: 59)

The transformation of the turntable into an instrument in the 1980s was not an aberration in the history of Black musical forms. Such inventive and disruptive uses of the turntable follow the dramatically innovative ways in which the mixing console was played like an instrument by various dub music innovators in 1970s Jamaica. In both cases, as with the steelpan in the 1930s, Afrological musical aesthetics and innovations invented new relations to modernity and its excesses. At our contemporary moment, the remix has emerged from various Afrosonic experimental musics as the dominant paradigm for musical innovation in popular music in the West (Veal 2007). Remixes as explored here signal a musical practice of altering an existing or prerecorded song, using both the addition and subtraction of lyrics, instrumentation and/or sound effects. Remixing, in relation to music, has been defined as 'taking samples from pre-existing materials to combine them to new forms according to personal taste' (Navas 2012). It is a more contemporary name for what sound systems were doing with versioning, what producers were doing with dub and what DJs such as Frankie Knuckles and Walter Gibbons were doing with turntables and reel to reels in the emergent house music and disco scenes respectively. Remixing using live music was first attempted by Jamaican music producers in the 1960s when they engaged in acts of versioning (Bradley 2000; Stolzoff 2000; Broughton and Brewster 2006; Veal 2007). Remix culture's precursors also firmly sit outside heteronormative dominant culture in the United States as the various DJ innovations in disco music made clear (Broschke 2011; Lawrence 2011).

As a music-making practice, it is not surprising to find that some of the earliest remix innovators were not from the mainstream. To remix is to at times break the rules, but more significantly remixing is about imagining and enacting other possibilities, while firmly holding in hand an existing reality – a precomposed and often already recorded song. Disco's acceptance and celebration of queer life pre-dated much of the mainstreaming of LGBTQ + culture one might find today on television and in popular culture. Music-making by Jamaicans existed literally and geographically on the periphery of the United States music industry, with acts such as the Wailing Wailers modelling themselves after Motown's slickly marketed groups like the Temptations until the influence of Rasta culture and aesthetics took hold.[1] Remixing as an act of poiesis productively engages the polyrhythmic and polyvocal nature of Afrosonic life – rather than privileging an ideal form or dominant narrative, all entanglements are at play. As a sonic innovation, remixing decomposes a song, releasing the multiple possibilities of any musical form and bringing together seemingly disparate ideas, materials and concepts to form a medium that can articulate the messiness and interconnectedness of contemporary life.

It has been more than a decade now since the explosion of remix culture on the academic scene, yet the level of scholarly debate remains underwhelmingly tied to the dominant discourses of Western culture. Lawyer Lawrence Lessig's *Remix: Making Art and Commerce Thrive in the Hybrid Economy*, published in 2008, and his earlier 2004 essay 'Free Culture' set the stage for the debates to come around remix culture. Writing from artistic communities, such as the *Horizon Zero* special issue on remix, published in French and from the Canadian context, were not very visible or well taken up despite being translated to English and being open source on the web. Scholars, such as Lessig and Lev Manovich, found ways to whitewash remix by ignoring Jamaica's historical role in this sort of sonic experimentation. These scholars were quick to bring remix

---

[1] See the imagery connected to the Wailer's first single, 'Simmer Down', to notice a short-haired Robert Nestor Marley nestled between Peter Tosh and Bunny Wailer.

culture into the dominant codes, overly obsessing with the legal implication of remixing and closing down its possibilities to do more than simply violate the tenets of North America's intellectual copyright regime (Lessig 2004; Manovich 2007). While other writers and scholars such as Virginia Kuhn, Margie Broschke, Erik Davis and Eduardo Navas engaged remix as a theoretical intervention by the 2010s, the early insights of DJ Spooky remain largely ignored or at best underappreciated. Severely lacking in many conversations around remix culture was its relation to non-Western musical precursors and the possibilities of otherness and difference as potential. Even further removed from many scholarly engagements were the legacies of Afrosonic experimentation and innovation from the days of Lee Scratch Perry, Errol Thompson, King Tubby and many others in Jamaican sound system culture, more than half a century ago. Ethnomusicologist Michael Veal's discussion of remix culture in *Dub: Shattered Soundscapes* did more to excavate the historical lineage and non-Western inheritances of remix than most scholars writing about remix in the early 2000s. Just like discussions of jazz decades ago, as George Lewis and Georgina Born rightfully point out, there remains an interesting way in which white critics and academics find ways to exonominate positionality and subsequently refuse to honour their entanglements (to be generous) with Black music and uphold the racial hierarchy (Born cited in Lewis 1996).

This chapter is attentive to dub music as a sonic innovation that offers a way of thinking about remix (and its entanglements) and its potential to unfinish musical objects and remain an open-ended system of significations. A focus on dub helps illuminate how contemporary remix culture is indebted to Jamaican sound system culture during the country's pre-independence growth of Indigenous musics in which copyright laws were not enforced (Brewster and Broughton 2014: 17). Sound systems were multigenerational – and in some circumstances family entrepreneurial endeavours, as was the case with Merritone Sound system, which garnered huge popular support and provided both an outlet for public enjoyment and a music industry development tool. Sound systems such as Duke Reid's Trojan Sound (as detailed in Chapter 1) were also instrumental in sonic innovation and experimentation that helped Jamaica's Indigenous music scene evolve (Chamberlain 2010).

I begin with a historical contextualization of dub and the remix as it builds on and extends sound system innovations from as far back as 1967. I then focus on three different kinds of remixes to demonstrate the potential impact of authorized and unauthorized remix practices, as well as an embodied praxis of the remix. In the final section, a dub mix of remix culture filters out the focus on intellectual property to accentuate and deepen possibilities of engaging a sonic subjectivity in which labour, time and oral aesthetics loosen the knowledge system that unpins dehumanization and racialization.

Dub, a signifying practice

Dub is a method of sound engineering and a compositional strategy in Jamaican sound system culture. It involves using the mixing console as an instrument to decompose and recompose songs by dropping vocals and instruments in and out of a track in spontaneous ways. In this process of altering a song, different instruments are echoed, sounds and lyrics are filtered and introduced in non-linear unpredictable patterns transforming a song into a fluid entity (Bradley 2000; Veal 2007). Timbre and texture are continually in flux, as each track is comprised of various instruments, sounds and phrases often processed through a reverb or echo chamber. As Veal suggests, at its most radical, dub's 'textual and syntactic qualities counteracted the dominance of westernized musical thinking' (2007: 16). The Dub Engineer's artistry sonically alters the 'original' composition, producing another version of a song. It was not uncommon for multiple versions of a track to be mixed, each done differently for a different sound system in the 1970s.[2] Veal's rigorous ethnographic work expands dub as a genre and expounds its significance in its own right and in relation to the global popularity of electronic music. His study provides excellent historizing of the musical landscape in Jamaican sound culture, building on this extensive fieldwork and the plethora of interviews and existing works that focus specifically on Jamaica.

Dubs originally referred to one-off acetates (eventually called dubplates) that were meant for previewing new music in the 1960s and the praise of an individual sound system in competitive sound clashes[3] (Barrow and Dalton

---

[2] See Tasha Rosez of Gunz & Rosez Sound System Dubplate Story Video Mix as she explains how she did not conceive of her sound as a real sound system until they obtained their own dubplates (Veal 2007).

[3] A sound clash is a competition between two or more sound systems. Now global in its reach, it is common to find sound clashes in various cities such as London, Toronto, Boston and Miami.

2004; Veal 2007; Chamberlain 2010; Sullivan 2013). Dubplates are prerecorded endorsements of a particular sound by a reggae artist; they usually follow the melody or lyrics of a popular tune (sometimes a tune sung by that same artist), inserting the name of the sound system and praise for that sound system's skills (Veal 2007; Chamberlain 2010). In some cases, these improvised lyrics for a dubplate would be cut as records and sold or added to albums (Bradley 2001; Veal 2007). In this sense, one can see dubplates as stimulating the recording industry by scouting and recording a variety of artists, a good portion of whom would develop careers. In the Jamaican music scene, various artists used the same instrumental backing, now called a riddim, to record their own version of an already existing song. Since the 'Mi Sleng Teng' riddim was released in 1985, it has become common for several artists to 'compete' on the same riddim instead of having their creativity stifled through endless litigation and sample clearance. In fact, at least 239 different recordings over the Sleng Teng riddim can be identified (Gilroy 1987). In this way, Jamaica's riddim method anticipated the concept of creative collaboration we currently see deployed in the Creative Commons debates today.

Dub has been described as 'raw riddim' by Prince Jammy, as it usually involves just the bass and the drums of a given track, minus the melody and instrumentation (Barrow and Dalton 2004). It has 'introduced the human ear to frequencies and soundwaves which were, hitherto, latent in some cases thus allowing for a different experience with musical notes, aural interpretations and space' (Howard 2016: 265). One of dub's most celebrated originators, King Tubby, an electronics genius who built his own amplifier with extraordinary bass capabilities, first began experimenting with studio mixing boards as instruments that could 'play' specific sounds within a track (Barrow and Dalton 2004). Phillip Maysles describes the 'Dub Organizer' as one that 'constructs aesthetic space through a process of removal, alteration, and layering' (Maysles 2002). In the process of creating a dub version, the engineer or 'Dub Organizer' extracts specific sounds or instruments and either eliminates or accentuates them using echo and reverb, to create sonic space. The Dub Organizer (the engineer/producer) strips a song down to just its drums and its bass and then proceeds to recompose the song in a different arrangement throughout the track.

In its deconstruction and reconstruction of songs, dub music demonstrates a specific ethic in working through and with sonic difference. In this encounter, the former commodity, the once enslaved African intercepts the linear progress narrative of the 'modern' via the technology – of the mixing board, in the case of dub (the turntable, in the case of hip-hop). Rather than passively accepting the structure of the song or the limits of the equipment, the actions of the Dub Organizer engage the structure and sonic properties of the song, creating multiple possibilities layered atop the drums and the bass using technology to extend grammars of Afrodiasporic orality and musical sensibility. The former commodity refuses the accepted use value of the mixing board and participates in remapping its functional possibilities. Instead of simply bringing two sounds together, the Dub Organizer seeks out a different sonic entity and crafts new and dynamic sonic textures, which imagine and reconfigure the mixing board as a musical instrument. The subjectivity proposed and enacted through the sonic experiment transforms one from being a unit of racialized labour to a co-author and agent of one's subjecthood when creating and elaborating the multiple possibilities of the sonic entity and the technological equipment. I read this as the former object's attempt to 'unfinish' entities, that is, to project the possibilities of exceeding one's socially proscribed limits, much like the work of the grand and petit marronage during centuries of enslavement. This notion or desire of multiple possibilities reveals a logic of creative participatory actions that create musics for the community's enjoyment, for competitive sport and for the fostering of a vibe, a sense of livity that exceeds Europe's racialized visual hierarchy. Like the self-styling of b-boys and b-girls, dub evidences an ethos of b-ing interested in extending the realm of the possible by participating in or co-authoring the meaning-making of the sonic realm.[4] DJ Spooky, one of the few early scholars of remix that acknowledged its Global South lineage, likes to think of Jamaican music culture as 'a shareware update, a software source for the rest of the world to upload' (Davis 2006).

Like the linguistic interventions of Rastafari explored earlier, dub operates through a mode of generous wandering, a 'give and take' that produces an aesthetic space which unfinishes projects in unpredictable ways (Glissant [1997] 2005). This logic, as well as its participatory desires and actions, can also be traced through current remix culture, where bootlegs[5] and mash-ups add to the ways in which digital culture has troubled calcified notions of the author

---

[4] Houston A. Baker's use of the term B-ing in his 1991 book, *Black Studies, Rap and the Academy* was an early and important reflection on how to think of hip-hop culture's subversive aesthetic impact.

[5] Bootlegs are largely understood as the unauthorized duplication of existing music or video material. See Rojas (2002).

and individual ownership. The suggestion 'no one owns sound' evidenced in dub's poetics is useful to extend to our thinking about the sole authorship of the dominant mode of being human. Dub tells us there is another logic of music-making that does not rely on extending Western musical thinking. This other logic is unbothered by copyright, invested in technical innovation and sonically aligned with expressions of African musical aesthetics.

Dub versions became commonplace within popular music as several non-reggae artists released B-side dubs, such as Madonna's Oakenfold Remix Dub for 'Celebration' in 2009 and Soul II Soul's Teddy Riley Rubba Dub mix for 'Keep on Movin'' a decade earlier in 1989.[6] Dub music then becomes the location of the playing out of a multiplicity that refuses a complete and isolated definition – it places in conversation different musicians, musical genres and time periods. In this line of thinking both Teddy Riley and Soul II Soul are authors of the 'Rubba Dub' version of 'Keep On Movin'' and Madonna and Paul Oakenfold both participate in the making of the house version of 'Celebration'. These multiple co-authors create versions, multiple possibilities for the engagement with their musical creations. Running counter to some of the more dominant forms of music composition in which individual 'genius' is revered, here I am thinking of classical music specifically; co-authors and deep collaboration expand on models of composition and signal the fading grasp of the solo, tortured musical prodigy or genius.

Contemporary engagements of the remix

Long before the music industry eagerly sought out remixes for their artists, avant-garde visual artists, such as Marcel Du Champ and Andy Warhol, engaged the concept of remixing; this involved recycling and recontextualizing objects, long before the contemporary terms of the remix were available. Terms, for instance version, cover song and dub, also littered musical landscapes before the language of the remix pervaded popular music in North America. Currently, remixing is an activity engaged largely by the technologically savvy, through which computer-based artists such as Girl Talk, Diplo and DJ Spooky invent their remixes. Remix culture has emerged in Western society as an ensemble

---

[6] See Madonna's 'Celebration' (Oakenfold 12" Dub), also see Soul II Soul's 'Keep on Movin'' B-side (Teddy Riley's Rubba Dub) Virgin Records 1989.

of recycling, borrowing and recontextualization that challenges current legal frameworks around private and exclusive ownership, corporate copyright culture and authorship (Lessig 2002, 2007; Boisvert 2003; Schütze 2003; Miller 2006; Reynolds 2009). For artists such as DJ Spooky or advocates of free culture, such as Creative Commons founder Lawrence Lessig, remix culture is about the free exchange of ideas and material culture as well as the battle against the tyranny of corporate ownership and copyright culture. The emerging language of 'configurable culture' and a general reading of remix as a fad negatively impact the popularization of serious ethical engagement with remix culture's antecedents and cultural intervention. Remix is more than the contemporary paradigm for music-making with analogue origins; it is not new, rather its digital manifestation, amplified by online internet-based tools, allows us to see more clearly this sonic innovation as elaborated across a number of fields.

Remixing has been a topic of debate in various circles outside of DJ culture, with analyses produced in documentaries, books and art exhibitions that provide an abundance of material engagements with this seemingly 'new' idea. The applicability of remixing now ranges far beyond musical creation, to include literature, films and a variety of visual content from the internet such as memes and TikTok videos. Importantly, prior to this explosion, Eduardo Navas delineated three types of musical remixes: the extended, the selective and the reflexive remix. The extended remix is longer than the original song and usually includes instrumental sections to make it more mixable for club DJs. The selective remix adds or subtracts parts of the original song. The reflexive remix 'allegorizes and extends the aesthetic of sampling, where the remixed version challenges the aura of the original and claims autonomy' (Navas 2012). Such a typology of remixes allows us to see the practice of remixing in a much more complex and artistic way, beyond its alleged copyright infringements. Further, and not part of Navas's original typology, is the cover song and its pedagogical possibilities, as the act of copying is also the act of learning. Of course, none of the typologies listed here are mutually exclusive, so a cover song or remake can be both a selective and an extended remix.

One of the first music remixes in North American popular culture is credited to Tom Moulton for his 1977 remix of MSFB's 'Love is the Message' (Broughton and Brewster 2006). As the pioneer of 12 inch records, and dance music remixes, Tom Moulton has a cult-like status in remix circles. Popular culture remixes – the heart of remix culture – consist of people utilizing computer technology to remix the most popular and danceable songs using various snippets, samples and instrumentals. Some of the most popular remix DJs rely heavily on what has been made possible by computer technology, such as the former chemical biologist (Greg Gillis) Girltalk, who cannibalizes popular musics and ravages popular memory to connect a string of popular sounds in new formations. Girltalk gained infamy for using a computer program to sample thirty seconds of popular songs and mix them together. He has been at the centre of a number of documentaries and legal controversies, as his practice of remixing conflicts with much of the musical establishment's reliance on the intellectual property rights regime in the United States. While not as politically outspoken as Lessig, Girltalk has been critical of the ways in which his practice has been negatively relegated and debased as theft.

In contrast to Girltalk's interest in navigating the legal constrictions of the music industry, DJ Spooky operates from a critical positionality in which his Black consciousness is embedded in his producing thought-provoking remixes in using music and videos. Spooky's work usually references political themes such as the film *Birth of a Nation*, or the Middle East conflict.[7] Consider, for example, a track on DJ Spooky's 'Ghost World Africa Now' remix, which he describes as being about 'polyrhythm and multiplex reality'. In one remix, DJ Spooky layers the vocals Nelson Mandela's 'Moments in Black History' over a popular hip-hop instrumental called 'Locked Up' by Senegalese-American Akon (Spooky 2007). This remix is both a didactic history lesson for the generation of youth who have only known a free Nelson Mandela and an attack on narrow categorization schemas that would like to think of politics and entertainment as separate or imagine a revolutionary and a rapper as two irreconcilable, unrelated and *unrelatable* entities. While entertainment and politics are not mutually exclusive, they are often kept separate in industry settings as a way to protect profits and not alienate consumers with varying levels of political awareness or concerns. Chronology and geography are disrupted by this remix, which utilizes the African diaspora's heterogeneity to pose a challenge to the insular ideas of nation that diaspora consistently disrupts and invalidates. The entire *Ghost World* mix, created by DJ Spooky to accompany his work in the 2007 Venice Biennale, takes listeners across the African continent and into the diaspora, bringing listeners into relation with a vast cross section of musics that illuminate the continent's musical diversity. DJ Spooky's music-based remixes are exemplary

---

[7] See Spooky (n.d.) for further details.

ways in which the politics of Black life and Black cultural production can be explored without overly focusing on legal constraints and industry profit metrics that overdetermine much of the public discourse on remix culture.

Since the early 2000s and the emerging debates around remix, various groups, beyond just artists and lawyers, have taken an interest in remixing. At the most simple and consumptive level, industries sought to capitalize on the popularity of the concept. For example, the Coca Cola Company's soft drink Sprite was one of the earliest brands to develop a drink called Tropical Sprite Remix in 2003. The soft drink featured fruit flavours mixed with the traditional lemon-lime carbonated drink. More recently, Nike offshoot, the Jordan Brand, created a series of shoes called the Jordan Fusions that utilize elements from different seasons of Air Jordan shoes and other popular Nike shoes and combine them into one shoe. Both companies, Nike and Coca Cola, sought use of the term and concept to market a type of newness to attract potential consumers.

Remix culture has proliferated across a number of fields and markets in a way that did not occur with dub music or other trends in the music industry. Historical context and geography are critical here as in the post-Napster moment (after 1998), with a generation of young people engaged in peer-to-peer culture and already familiar with the concept of a remix from popular music, remix culture could emerge en masse, beyond just its original musical context. Rather than the concept of remix remaining contained within music circles as dub remained in the 1970s onwards, digital culture and more accessible home computers with internet service (in the Global North) catapulted remixing into the middle of youth popular culture where cool hunting corporations were quick to co-opt. Despite this reality, and somewhat prior to corporate infiltration, artist communities nicely wrestled with the remix at the level of the idea, emphasizing possibilities rather than legal restrictions.

A few artist-led events have interrogated the potentialities of the remix concept to the world of art and identity: a roundtable discussion, called 'Remix and Feedback', held at the Emily Carr Institute in 2004; an exhibition and roundtable called *The Mix: Conversations on Creolization and Artist Community Collaborations* at A-Space Gallery in Toronto in 2004; and a travelling exhibition called *Remix: New Modernities in a Post Indian World* in 2008.[8] At the 'Remix

---

[8] *Remix: New Modernities in a Post Indian World* exhibited at the National Museum of the American Indian, Smithsonian Institute in Washington, DC, the Heard Museum in Phoenix, the Art Gallery of Ontario in Toronto and the George Gustav Heye Center, National Museum of the American Indian in New York City.

and Feedback' roundtable, the remix was envisioned as a way to resist cultural passivity and become more assertive around our identities, while other panellists cautioned against forging the creation of new cultural models (Lai 2004). The tone of the panel, as reported by Adrienne Lai, moved between caution over government control and corporate control. One panellist provocatively proposed himself to be the embodiment of the remix, personifying his post-identity politics as a person of mixed racial ancestry. Lai's overall assessment of the panel, despite its failure to address gender, was that they understood the remix as a useful tool of resistance against dominant narratives and a way of 'interrogating narratives and owning memory' (Lai 2006: 2).

The Mix, curated by Andrea Fatona, was not an explicit interrogation of the concept of remix. Rather it was an opportunity to have a diasporic exploration of creolization, hybridity and transculturation. This exhibit and roundtable was interested in taking up issues of identity amongst Caribbean and Caribbean Canadian populations and sought to explore alternative discourses of multi-ethnic life that lay beyond Canadian state policy. In Honor Ford-Smith's review of the event, she highlights the hyphened, multiple identities that belong to a social group called 'Caribbeans' (Ford-Smith 2004: 2). By moving from the abstract levels of transculturation, hybridity and creolization to the lived experiences of students, emigrants and Canadian-born individuals in Toronto, Ford-Smith suggests how we might understand an embodied notion of the (re)mix. The invention of a new social group called the 'Caribbeans' that Ford-Smith hints at is an important opportunity to reflect on the role of the Caribbean in bringing theory to the ground to examine how these theories live within people. By actively taking up the remix, these artists bring into crisis much of society's foundational ideas. Western societies have not been constructed to accommodate the contradictory lives of those in-between.[9] As Adrienne Lai suggested and the *Remix* exhibit demonstrated, remixing interrogates narratives, highlighting the contradictory ways the West socially and discursively constructs and obscures to its advantage. Such public debate and discourse around remix largely lived outside of the more popular and less provocative market-aligned uses of the idea of the remix. What these artists demonstrate with their willingness to wrestle with the concept is to widen the discursive terrain and open up possibilities

---

[9] We just have to think of the kinds of social disruption made possible by racially mixed individuals from Louis Riel to Frida Kahlo to Frederick Douglass and Vicente Guerrero.

for thinking about the remix outside of market relations. For them, remix was engaged in a generative intellectual debate, a way to think out of sync with dominant ideas around identity and race.

The practice of remixing troubles much of our present systems of knowledge construction and subjectivities because it pivots on a relational logic that seeks connection rather than the siloed disconnection that masks Eurocentric power relations. Remixes are the past, present and future combined. They rely on memories, nostalgia and the past as equally as the present, the experiential portion of the sonic experiment and now the evolution of digital technology. According to one assessment, remix music 'organizes collective memories' from other times and places, allowing us to engage the various routes, territories and times that constitute the diasporic experience – across races and ethnicities (Maira 2000: 334).

Contextualizing the remix this way connects the various Afrosonic innovations to the realities of cultural production in the African diaspora as something more than entertainment or fodder for the creative industries. The refusal here is to read remixing as more than solely entertainment, as also an activity that moves across various domains of Western life including as an episteme that produces knowledge about Black living (Baker 1993; Woods 2007; Henriques 2011).

Dubbing the remix

Since dub can be understood as the stripping of a musical track so that it becomes just the drums and the bass, it is useful to utilize this technique to strip the concept of the remix down to its essence, before the word remix was sayable. At its core, remix is about the negotiation of difference, the interruption of sameness and the centrality of reception in the creative process. Much of the popular discourse around remixing, especially outside the art gallery, has been deeply disconnected from Black life, possibly owing to the ways in which the visual identifiers of race are not necessary coordinates to derive meaning from a remix. To suture this disconnection, I turn to studies around orality. Walter J. Ong's take on narrative originality amongst 'cultures with high oral residue' (Ong 1982) helps us think about remix culture as a form of cultural production that is connected to the enslaved African populations in the West as one of the New World's oral cultures. Ong's quote at the opening of this chapter highlights a way in which we might understand remixing as a logic related to the world view of non-Western cultures. Take, for example, any of the Brer Rabbit folklore or Anansi the spider tales in which the animal characters change, but the moral of the tale remains the same, foregrounding tricksterism and the evading or exercising of power.

If narrative originality, as Ong suggests, is about managing one's interaction with an audience through reshuffling existing narrative material, what becomes clear is that the practice of versioning and, eventually, remixing is an extension of this practice. Remixing as a form of narrative originality that pre-dates Western industries' intellectual property rights, illuminates how a narrative of non-Western peoples can be generatively disruptive to our status quo as reproduced by scholars examining remix culture in the late 2000s.

If we understand remixing as an activity invested in participating and restructuring or re-narrating the dominant codes of our present moment, then we can draw a connection between remixing and notions of liberation that lie beyond the 'freedom' rhetoric of liberal humanism. At the level of the idea, even before it becomes discourse or materializes physically or sonically, remixing involves an open participatory structure, invested in democratic enunciations and the disruptive potential of forging newness out of present circumstances/materials. I work here with dub poetics as theoretical tools to disorganize and make strange the uses and contemporary notions of the remix so as to decipher its inner workings that produce new meanings and loosen the grasp of hegemonic Western knowledge systems. The goal here is to amplify, echo and reverberate the connective relational aspects of remixing and to filter out the discourses around the Western concepts of copyright infringement and personal property. The usefulness of the debates around copyright and originality is that they signal a crisis of the author – an important breach into Western thought systems still stuck on notions of individual property rights.

Rather than present us with new material in the sense that we experience pictures and songs created from scratch, remixing is about reshuffling, bricolage and recontextualizing already existing materials into a new arrangement, in a new aesthetic formation. In diffusing the hegemony of the notion of the single author, erected alongside the ascendence of the individual in Western thought according to Barthes, the remix refuses the supremacy of the individual and actively rejects the hermeneutically sealed silos of Western thought. Dub mixes have multiple authors both in the production on a specific song and in the presentation of the song by a sound system. The manner in which a dub or any musical track is played in a dance hall session is influenced by the dancing audience as cheers, waving hands and calls for a wheelback (as explored in Chapter 1) create a sonic environment formed collaboratively in relation.[10] These versions, where call and response, the wheelback and other forms of repetition are present tell us the European conception of the author is a provincial, limited and contingent notion codified by colonial power and written into law. In the moment when crowds yell out 'dubwise' in their call to the sound system for the riddim track or instrumental version of a song, the notion of the author is already dead and being remixed in real time when the Selector responds with the version requested by the audience.

The remix unravels the politics of its constitution; it is only recognizable as a remix because people can recognize its parts, such as its original tracks or sampled instrumentation (Navas 2012). To utilize a conception of the remix as a disruptive intervention, I operationalize remixing as a deciphering practice, one that highlights systems of meaning and attempts a 'transvaluation of values' (Wynter 1992). To understand remixing as a deciphering practice – a cultural critique – is to first refuse the artificial consumer/creator dichotomy that deeply restricts the possibilities of humans to the realm of solely biological, not creative agents in the narrativization of their existence. The remix reveals the possibilities of human agency in narrating and re-narrating one's reality against and beyond the consumer subjectivity posed and reinforced by the dominant codes of Western capitalism. Further, while the aesthetics and poetics of remixing can be stimulating and produce pleasure, the work here is to illuminate the structures, discourses and spaces of strategic intervention that the remix facilitates at the level of the idea.

Pivoting on a value system based on creative collaboration, reuse and recycling, remixing refuses static and hegemonic meaning – as such it can challenge the meaning and value of all it engages. At stake here is the potential of remixing and its associated thought processes to disrupt systems of meaning-making by separating 'social and material production' from 'cultural production' (Wynter 1992). This process, then, of remixing as a deciphering practice, places special emphasis on the demystification of the rhetorical discursive manoeuvres of the dominant logic that make genre (in the case of music) a rigid and 'natural' system of categorization. Further, to bring together remix culture and notions of 'freedom' in Western liberal discourse is to return to the notion of participation/

---

[10] The actions of the Selector or DJ after receiving a response from the crowd enters into a dialogue, one that influences the actions of the person controlling the music.

creative labour, not consumption, as an act of liberation beyond the rhetoric of 'freedom'. Since remixing is a form of cultural production that loosens the vice grip of Homo oeconomicus, its creative ethos can be said to initiate or reactivate human agency as an operational modality of human rationality not centred on the visual supremacy embedded in Eurocentric thought. To separate cultural production from social and material production is to begin to ask what is the work of the remix, or what can the remix discursively interrupt or gesture towards?

The works of artists, once separated from the social and material forces that shape Western society, present us with ideas and practice not offered by the dominant logic. The space of music has been the site where innovation, experimentation and counter-world views are manifested, particularly for oppressed communities because of the tactics of racial exclusion (Wynter 1977; McRobbie 1999). It is against and beyond the racializing ocular logic that dehumanizes non-white humans that we begin to glimpse multiple human formations that move away from ideal man or Man 0.0 on McKittrick's graphic representation (McKittrick 2015). These forms are not (at least initially) market-orientated and do not reproduce the logics of exclusion evidenced in the bourgeois 'ideal' man. Indeed, the forms of sonic subjectivity suggested by those engaged in remix music can be read beyond the dominant 'freedom as consumption' logic as existing in a realm of rationality exercising an opacity to the dominant forms. Thus, the ideas that informed sound systems earliest experimentations with the version and dubplates were innovations fuelled by a desire for sonic dominance in the competitive arena of sound, not solely about the accumulation of capital – a logic DJ Kool Herc would use to develop his massive speakers in New York City in the years before hip-hop emerged as a commercial entity. Importantly, one of the metrics of success for a sound system is the enjoyment of the people – the invention of sonic subjectivities to transform the labouring body (via kinaesthetic and oral interventions) into more-than-'Man'.

If we return to the relationship between the enslaved individual and the enslaver, the idea of narrative originality and the continual destabilizing of the narrative of enslavement via grand and petit marronage suggest a deeper reconsideration of how we might imagine the conceptual yield of the remix. The various forms of resistance captured in the historical literature on transatlantic slavery, from poisonings to flight, suggest we might think about the enslaved individual's various forms of resistance as efforts to recontextualize the narrative (if we can think of one's lived experience as a narrative) of ownership and enslavement. If we return to the pivotal scene in Frederick Douglass's narrative, when he battles Mr Covey, resistance, as a recontextualization of one's narrative, is made clear. 'You seen how a man was made a slave, you shall see how a slave was made a man' (Douglass 1993: 75) is how Douglass begins his two-hour physical battle with the 'nigger breaker' Edward Covey. Douglass describes his success in this battle as a pivotal 'epoch in my humble history' (75). This confrontation, as part of Douglass's personal journey to freedom, is representative of the narrative of the enslaved and their disruption of the systems that regulated their socially sanctioned oppression.

The relationship between owner and the enslaved individual, then, was constantly retold, recontextualized and re-narrated by Maroon communities such as Ganga Zumba in Quilombo dos Palmares or Nanny in Cockpit Country. Was this attempt to re-author the narrative of enslavement the original remix? Is such a question even useful? Rather than search for origins, I am interested in how the relational identity of enslaved individuals fostered various forms of identification. Maroon subjectivity plots a human form outside of, yet adjacent to, the plantation and outside of the sphere of influence of bourgeois society. Did enslaved populations experience a double consciousness, the constant shifting between subject and object? The numerous histories of rebellion and revolution suggest that commodity status was a temporal and hegemonic identity that was constantly transgressed. At the point of contact, where Africa meets Europe, creolization theory suggests the existence of an infinite number of possible outcomes (Burton 1995; Glissant 1997). Remixing, then, can be thought of as the productive possibilities of the encounter, or the collision, where two or more systems of knowledge and values interact or intertwine.

Beyond copyright regimes

The multiple possibilities created and negotiated in polyrhythmic African musics move us in a direction to re-examine remixing as something more than the dominant logic, particularly in relation to Afrodiasporic life. The notion of the mix found in DJ culture is one useful strategy to think about the complex ways in which sound relates to the experiences of Afrodiasporic peoples. The mix is a temporary moment of transition where the DJ attempts to introduce a new record to their audience by matching the tempo of the existing, or currently playing, record. In this temporal moment, beats per minute are matched as the drums and snares (on the one and the three) of the new song are layered on top of, or mixed into, the existing sounds; in essence, it is the 'interfacing of different grooves' into a new 'totality' (Weheliye 2005).

Theoretically, such circumstances have been elaborated by Afrofuturist thinkers such as Kwodo Eshun and DJ Spooky in works such as *More Brilliant than the Sun* (1998) and *Rhythm Science* (Miller 2004) respectively. As highlighted by these two thinkers, the concept of the mix lends itself to theorization when it is understood as a 'multivalent temporal structure', which produces seamless interpolations between objects to 'fabricate a zone of representation' (Miller 2004, 2006). Beyond a technical understanding, mixing and remixing illuminates the activity of negotiating multiple possibilities, recombinant realities and the creative modes necessary to reimagine the rearrangement of one's existential reality.

The logic of remixing borrows and extends the cut 'n' mix notion Hebdige illuminated in his important book, *Cut 'N' Mix: Culture, Identity and Caribbean Music* (1987). Hebdige recognized an operational logic outside of ownership and intellectual property rights utilized to deal with the limited musical possibilities of Jamaica's post-1958 music scene and the limited electronic possibilities of the mid 1970s, when dub musical innovations exploded in popularity (Veal 2007). The idea at the core of remixing – that no one owns a sound – is one way to begin thinking about what (beyond the creative freedom fostered by the lack of legal repercussions) structures the ideational possibilities embedded in dub's sonic experiments.

We can examine further what remixes do by looking more closely at different music remixes that demonstrate aspects of the practice of remixing. When commercially driven, remixes can expose artists to new audiences, especially when merging two different genres of music as was the case with the Aerosmith & Run DMC's video collaboration for their 1986 cover of Aerosmith's 1975 song 'Walk This Way'. When fan-driven or artist-driven remixes arise, while they have the potential to become commercial entities, their value lies in the wide and generous interpretations fan and artists add to their remixes. In what follows, I move through three different kinds of remixes found in works that do more than expand audiences or shore up the priorities of industry-based stakeholders. By examining three different remixes of music by Public Enemy, K'naan and M.I.A., the multiple possibilities of remixing open generative and generous ways to capture how the signifying practices of a remix decipher our governing codes and productively breach the established intellectual property regime.

Released in 1992, Public Enemy's 'Shut 'Em Down' is a lyrically charged example of boom bap hip-hop in its most politicized form. Socially conscious in its scathing critique of American society and the lack of corporate social responsibility, this track was the fourth single from their album *Apocalypse 91: The Enemy Strikes Back*. The track begins with Terminator X's baby scratches prior to the first beat enhancing the downbeat. His next scratch is a stab, slowly releasing the prerecorded sound of an electric guitar and continuously alternating various scratches of the electric guitar sample; from stabs to double-time baby scratches, the scratch is a prominent aspect of the track's musical aesthetic and central compositional feature. The texture of the track is structured by DJ Terminator X's significant scratching throughout the song, and accentuated in a solo in the final minute of the track as Chuck D's rhymes trails off to become ad libs. This has the effect of centring Public Enemy's DJ's skills, reminding us of the earlier years of hip-hop culture before the emcee was the centre of attention. The chorus of the song, utilizing both Chuck D and Flavour Flav's voices repeats the song's title, allowing for a breakdown at 3:53 to showcase Terminator X's scratches. This adherence to the foundational aesthetic of hip-hop's golden era of boom bap by focusing on the DJ allows 'Shut 'Em Down' to resonate with its existing fan base, one whose tastes migrated in the 1980s and 1990s from breaks and funk records commonplace a decade earlier in the culture, to a slower more bass driven Roland 808 kick drums.

The official remixed version of 'Shut 'Em Down' was produced by a relatively new producer at the time, the now legendary Pete Rock. Now, some thirty years later, Pete Rock is considered a leading figure in hip-hop production and an inspiration to the much celebrated, the late James Yancey, aka J Dilla, architect of the humanizing of digital drums. In the Pete Rock remix of 'Shut 'Em Down', he redesigns the mood and texture of the track by removing a number of elements from the original. Terminator X's plethora of exemplary scratches (whose repetition strings together the track with a certain continuity) are replaced by a rolling horns sample repeating continuously throughout the entire track. While Chuck D's lyrics remain completely intact, the Pete Rock remix version slows down the track to 91 bpm. The new tempo of the track accomplishes at least two things. Firstly, the track now becomes more easily mixed into sets by DJs in that era as bpms in the ninety to ninety-five range were commonplace in the early 1990s. This possibility moves the track from suitable for home play and personal Walkmans to widening its possible play in party settings and clubs where DJs might be mixing tracks.

Secondly, Pete Rock's new tempo removes the staccato feel of Terminator X's scratches and allows for greater malleability of the horns, which now structure the track. The sampled horns are looped in an eight-bar formation, modelling the track around one of the sounds normalized in tracks produced by the Bomb Squad,[11] possibly signifying homage from the emerging producer to the reigning hip-hop production team of the times. The looping eight bars of the horn sample descend in volume, producing a siren effect, as if an emergency vehicle is driving away from the listener, only to return at full volume and again upfront in the track. Like the many ways in which dub engineers would bring sounds in and out of the mix, here Pete Rock's sampling technique manipulates the volume of the sample throughout the track, a technique that produces a sonic illusion of movement and distance.

Another aesthetic feature of this remix is the use of the producer's voice to echo the main vocal elements of the track. In replacing Flavour Flav's echoing of Chuck D on the chorus, Pete Rock uses repetition and echo on both his horn sample and his vocal accompaniment of the track. In using his voice, Pete Rock employs a technique of stuttering as he echoes the chorus, something we see today in songs by Kanye West (prior to the era of autotune). But importantly, we cannot disconnect Pete Rock's innovation on the microphone from the ways in which DeeJays such as U-Roy and Count Machucki would improvise sounds in relation to the gaps and instrumentation in the music. In the original version of the track, Flavour Flav's repetition of the song's title as he backs up Chuck D's vocals mimics the aesthetics of sampling, pronouncing only the beginning of the phrase, repeating 'shut 'em, shut 'em shut 'em'. The end of the phrase, 'down', is said only in alignment with the downbeat to maintain rhythmic flow. Pete Rock employs a stutter technique to truncate the phrase until only the sound of shhh is repeated thrice in rhythmic flow until the end of the four-bar beat in which the entire phrase is said. The residues of orality are significant here, as musical gestures and features blur and unite musical and oral aesthetics.

The Pete Rock remix for 'Shut 'Em Down' is an authorized, legal creation, released by Def Jam records with all of its samples cleared. Its sonic gestures

---

[11] The Bomb Squad is a production trio originally consisting of brothers Keith and Hank Shocklee and Eric Sadler. The team's sound of highly collaged samples, sometimes hundreds per track, formed the bedrock of the Public Enemy sound.

and techniques, while grounded in hip-hop sampling aesthetics, demonstrate the enduring influence of dub music on sampling and remix aesthetics. This remix accomplishes a significant mood change in the track by changing the track's instrumentation while maintaining all of the socially conscious lyrics of this protest song. The track increases its sense of urgency with the addition of the looping eight-bar horn sample while extending its appeal to dancing audiences operating at more mixable beats per minute. As a legally authorized industry approved remix, Pete Rock's version of 'Shut 'Em Down' is an example of a selective remix, with the additions and subtractions of specific sounds, neither extending the length of the track nor challenging the original aura of the track. One might argue that this track plays a significant role in the launching or amplification of the producer's career as a high-profile display of Pete Rock's early career sampling prowess.

As an industry approved remix and financially resourced, the track demonstrates what is possible within the rules of the copyright regime. Most importantly, this remix exemplifies how difference and sameness can be brought together in a track as the change of instrumentation rests comfortably alongside the original lyrics, listeners are encouraged to hold in tension sameness and difference in reconciling another version of this song.

In stark contrast to this well-funded industry-approved remix is the internet-circulated and unfunded cover track remix 'Dayless Night', which features no new production and no clear connection to the music industry, in what is believed to be an unauthorized remix by Somali-born, Canadian-based emcee K'naan of American artist Kid Cudi's first commercially successful single, 'Day 'N Nite' released in 2009.

'Dayless Night' unauthorized/unreleased remix

Kid Cudi's success from 'Day 'N' Nite' owes much to its lyrics, tales of a stoner's high, loneliness and an erratic trip. Sonically, the track was on the cutting edge of popular music in 2009, as it borrowed heavily from electronic music, an aspect amplified by the Crookers remix, which was licensed and obtained its own official video. K'naan, an emcee, emerged out of Toronto with a track called 'Soobax' in 2005, which sought to call out warlords in Somalia, using the Somali language for his title and chorus. While the track is titled in the Somali language, K'naan rhymes the track in English. Much of K'naan's work has been what I have called elsewhere a diasporic disruption, an indictment of North American commercial hip-hop's overly violent posturing using his life experiences in Somali as his tool of critique (Rana and Campbell 2020).

'Dayless Night' in its compositional structure varies from Pete Rock's remix discussed above. In borrowing from Manuel and Marshall's 'riddim method' concept in relation to reggae and reggaeton, the track is a re-voicing of Kid Cudi's hit track. The recycling of instrumental riddims, has been a feature of music-making for at least half a century, since the days of dubplates in 1960s and 1970s Jamaica. While in the context of the United States, Kid Cudi's instrumental for 'Day 'N' Nite' was not circulated widely as would be the case amongst producers such as King Jammy. Instead, K'naan takes a decidedly non-Western approach to riffing off Kid Cudi's success and employs a remix that borrows from Jamaica's rich musical legacy and appears to work outside of the constraints of copyright rules.

In K'naan's aptly titled remix, 'Dayless Night', he provides his own revised lyrics over Cudi's original beat, choosing to amplify the plight of Somali pirates and the less-than-ideal reality of Mogadishu since the fall of the country's government in 1991. At the very outset of the track, K'naan speaks directly to Cudi thanking him for the 'paddle' and claiming to 'borrow this real quick'.

Lyrically, K'naan proceeds to dislodge the original meaning of Cudi's song, a very North American weed-smoking adventure. K'naan rhymes the chorus:

> dayless nights, I see pirates in the ocean late at night
> they roam around and can't wait to fight,
> watch out for pirates roaming late at night (at at at night).

Revising Kid Cudi's original chorus:

> Cuz day and night
> The lonely stoner seems to free his mind at night,
> He's all alone through the day and night,
> The lonely loner seems to free his mind at night (at at at night).

Cudi's very personal and individualist narrative structure is revamped by K'naan decidedly non-Western perspective. He invests himself in the pirate's pain, describing the situation off the coast of Somalia from the perspective of a pirate. In taking on this perspective, K'naan is able to provide a level of intimacy by humanizing these otherwise not well-known individuals. In describing his tip-toeing over landmines and avoiding bomb blasts, K'naan refuses the dominant narratives of Black life in the West and instead focuses on the realities of decades-long war that has ravaged the formerly unified country of his birth.

In the second verse of his remix, K'naan switches his narrative style moving from the perspective of a pirate to another vantage point that warns of pirate ships at night. K'naan's remix works to leverage the popularity of Cudi's debut song to provide the West with perspectives on the lives and humanity of the Somali pirates. The 'Day 'N' Nite' instrumental provides K'naan with a way to rely on the familiarity of the popular song to get the attention of the audiences he seeks to attract, mainly the English-speaking West. The priority of his political message ensured his lyrical revisions to the track followed a similar rhyming pattern, with repetition in the chorus and pauses to create space for emphasis at the end of rhyming couplets.

This seemingly unauthorized or unofficial remix, in contrast to the Crookers remix, illuminates how the creative labour of re-voicing is expressed in contemporary hip-hop and pop music. Further, in taking into consideration the media cycle in the West, and the ways in which the reporting of Somali pirates relies on their othering and criminalization, this unauthorized remix provides an unfiltered perspective, signifyin' on the meaning of piracy in the post-Napster context. K'naan engages in piracy while humanizing Somali deemed as pirates by the mainstream media. The cleverness of K'naan's wordplay, steeped in rhyming couplets, pauses and repetition allow for the conveyance of a deeply political message that ruptures dominant Western notions of Black life, particularly in the Global South. This versioning of Cudi's popular debut track brings forward lineages of Afrosonic innovations to do the work of providing a minority, Somali perspective on an international geopolitical struggle. Like DJ Spooky's *Ghost World* mix, K'naan's remix's potential is one of the amplification of political messages and the leveraging of existing platforms and technologies to insert and prioritize concerns that revolve around more than just profit margins and returns on investment. Both the authorized Pete Rock remix and the unofficial K'naan remix zoom in on how contemporary remixes provide a method to decipher and re-author Black life by using creative labour to gesture towards new relations that exceed the rigidly protected boundary between political consciousness in contemporary popular music.

Prior to K'naan's 2009 remix and his act of signifyin' on the doubly problematic circulation of pirates and piracy, the mixtape 'Piracy Funds Terrorism' landed into the hands of fans at M.I.A. concerts and made its way onto the internet in 2004. On this unauthorized mixtape, emerging producer (now globally known) DJ Diplo remixes eight tracks featuring an unknown artist using the name M.I.A. She entered the global music scene via a mixtape distributed for free on the internet and sampling verses and instrumentals from a wide variety of hip-hop and dancehall artists. Without legal clearance, the mixtape did not get an official release but was highly influential in bringing M.I.A. into the popular music scene in North America as early versions of her songs on this mixtape made it onto her debut album. Importantly, one track featuring lyrics from L.L. Cool J's 'Headsprung' had to be removed from the mixtape, possibly due to a dispute with a record label. Listening carefully to the samples and ad libs between tracks, one can read this mixtape in deep conversation with Jamaican sound system culture. At 8:08 in the mixtape, the sampled ad libs include a female voice saying 'strictly rockers' and a Mikey Dread sample toasts over the Bam Bam riddim, popularized by Tanto & Metro's 'Murder She Wrote'; the listener is treated to a classic rhyming couplet doubled at the end of phrase:

> A Dread at the controls,
> international controller throughout the world
> universal beat marshall/we no partial
> we play dubwise selection with no objection.

The word 'objection' echoes out repeating another five times before Diplo speeds up the riddim to begin mixing in the next track. This usage of echo is utilized multiple times throughout the mixtape, channelling the innovations of King Tubby, Errol Thompson and the generation of dub innovators that clearly continue to influence contemporary electronic music. With the riddim method employed in extended ways on mixtapes, the unauthorized usage of various lyrics, samples and instrumentals form the bedrock for the invention of new relations that can illuminate other kinds of political and social futures.

The case of M.I.A. provides another interesting variation of remixing as a sonic innovation, and more specifically in her oral and aesthetic styling. Yet, just like K'naan and Public Enemy, her body of musical works are deeply political and refuse the separation of popular culture and politics. With London-born Sri Lanka-raised visual and recording artist M.I.A., it is apparent that much of the conceptual yield of dub and remix can provide a praxis for living social and racial difference. As a recording artist, M.I.A. has been the perfect embodiment of the remix posited in the 2004 'Remix and Feedback' panel and Andrea Fatona's *The Mix* exhibition. Using the sonic stylings of Jamaican toasting, hip-hop vernacular and referencing her Tamil and South London routes, M.I.A. exploded onto the music scene in 2004. Her uncategorizable hybrid style has been described as 'mish-mashed, electro-ragga groove and conscious couplets' (Collins 2005).

Her first commercial single is telling of her remix sensibility. 'Galang' is a mixture of the Jamaican patwa phrase 'ga long' and the name of the South Asian ginger root galangal. 'Galang' and several other tracks on her debut album feature eclectic oscillations, echoes and refractions of Jamaican patwa, American hip-hop vernacular and South London slang. M.I.A. echoes London's playful mixes of Jamaican sound system culture that began with the import of ska and development of two tone (Heathcott 2003), but her Sri Lankan upbringing reverbs this transatlantic crossing of sound. In her work, we are treated to intentionally hybrid stylings, such as the opening line of 'Sunshowers': 'I bongo with my lingo, and beat it like a wing yo / From Congo to Colombo, can't stereotype my thing yo' (2005). M.I.A's diasporic wandering across genre, continent and racial boundaries allow her music to resonate with a number of 'markets' making it difficult to categorize her. Her explanation of her style is simple, 'I just try to reflect how we live today', 'you get exposed to everything. I'm kind of like a walking mixtape' (M.I.A. cited in Empire 2005).

M.I.A. echoes Glissant's chaos-monde theorization; refracting through the language of hip-hop culture, her very espousal of her style demonstrates an interconnected diasporic sensibility that refuses to obey the barriers of language, culture or nation and opts instead to make artistic the collision between Global North and Global South, between Black musical aesthetics and South Asian cultures. Instead of isolating her grasp of remix culture to a single track, one can find hybrid and recombinative styling across a number of domains in her work from dance to lyrics. For example, in the video for 'Paper Planes', M.I.A. sports hefty gold rope chains beneath a huge black hooded jacket reminiscent of 1980s New York hip-hop artists such as Rakim and RUN DMC, while in another scene she sports a vintage Metallica T-shirt. She moves through scenes not imbued with social capital such as the pirated DVD shop, the subway and the food truck. Sonically, in 'Paper Planes' M.I.A.'s producers recontextualize the gunshot into the rhythmic flow of the track, repeating the sample five times on the last four bars of her eight-bar chorus punctuated with the sound of an opening cash register on the final beat. As a celebratory song, rather than an ethnographic detail of pain and death, the gunshot sample can be read as a homage to the celebrated sound of gunshots mimicked by enthusiastic dancehall audiences whose sonic allusion recursively brings Duke Reid's sound system legacy into the present.

Like the dub organizer, M.I.A. snatches various aspects of her lived soundscape (her narrative) and remixes these phrases, sounds and styles, leading to descriptions of her sound as 'new and boundless' (McKinnon 2005) and as 'explod[ing] the precious small-mindedness of national and generic divides' (Jennings 2006). Instead of using her various encounters with other cultures as ammunition for the oppression or eradication of social difference, or the rehearsal of the narrative of Black death hastily consumed by mainstream America, M.I.A. becomes a creative collaborator in the articulation of her hybrid and globalized narrative. In her videos, she centres racialized people and refuses to present the female body as scantily clad for visual consumption. In her various interruptions of national boundaries and musical genres, she also refuses to separate the political from entertainment and thus firmly situates herself within Black expressive traditions. M.I.A. named her first album *Arular*, after her father's secret code name in the fight for a free Tamil Eelam when he battled alongside the Eelam Revolutionary Organization of Students. She has also been very outspoken in regards to the Sri Lankan conflict involving the Tamil Tigers (Baron 2009). Her genre-bending newness brought her heightened attention, which provides for a platform where poverty, prostitution and the oppression of minority populations can be heard on an international scale. Here M.I.A. reminds us of Somali-Canadian emcee K'naan and his multiple stylings that both reference and resist North American hip-hop culture, filtering their politically poignant messaging to resonate aesthetically in relation to legacies of hip-hop and dancehall music and culture. M.I.A. embodies the remix aesthetic taking a dub-like decomposing method to elements of popular culture and recomposing a sonic and visual articulation of another, more heterogenous relation based in values much more generously conceived than the bourgeois ideals of European culture.

Dubwise/Dub wisdom

In inventing the high-pass filter and experimenting with the creation of echo using two tape recorders, King Tubby invented methods and tools to actively decompose and recompose music. While many of his techniques are commonplace in various music scenes, from electronica to pop music, today they are built directly into DAWs. The recomposition and recombinative possibilities invented by dub pioneers teach us to live with difference as a state of becoming and that homogeneity and heterogeneity can coexist. As Michael Veal reminds us, dub mixing strategies foregrounded fragmentation and incompletion, strategies that make the modern-day remix possible. Dub remixing techniques provide templates for the creation of spatial and textual experimentations undoing and loosening the record for other realities and sonic possibilities.

The meaning created in each new remixed version is inscribed within a system of references, playing upon past meanings while building its current meaning through excessive referencing of prior versions. This sonic activity represents future thoughts as it makes productive the unforeseen aspects of the encounter between different musics, discourses and memories. The remix as an Afrosonic innovation evidences a sonic variety of Glissant's systematic/archipelagic thought, which he describes as 'another form of thought is developing, more intuitive, more fragile, threatened, but in sync with the chaos-world and the unforeseeable' ([1997] 2005: 119). As sonic innovations like remixing continue to materialize cultural relations that disrupt our status quo, their importance is doubled by their reliance on sound and not solely on the visual realm to accomplish another articulation, a more multisensory rendition of our present moment.

Following Glissant's notion of 'culture as totality' and 'chaos-monde', which he defines as the 'immeasurable intermixing of cultures' (Glissant 1997), remixing as a conceptual tool takes on added significance when we begin to read it as a tool of decipherment. M.I.A., as the embodiment of the remix, not only illuminates the very limited notions of genre prevalent in popular music but also aligns with a politically conscious way of both engaging her culture and a socially conscious way of working with Black musical culture that work to ethnically disrupt and not reproduce the depoliticized and extractive tendencies of the mainstream music industry. The act of remixing then refuses to abide by the boundaries of our present organization of music, cultures, thoughts and memories. K'naan, Public Enemy and M.I.A. (amongst many others, of course) ensure a political consciousness lives in their music despite the limitations of a popular music industry. Remixing deciphers how cultural production, when not deeply enmeshed in the social and material regimes of the dominant culture, might produce other kinds of aesthetic value schemas, minoritized perspectives and systems of meaning that generously invest in well-being. The work the remix does, then, illuminates the seams of a fabricated isomorphic Western life. The remixes explored here, only a sliver of the thousands of political and apolitical songs in existence, suggest minority perspective on human well-being can coexist within mainstream industries and the act of remixing takes us beyond the silos and structures that maintain an entrenched model of capital accumulation at the cost of human well-being.

In terms of intellectual property, remix deciphers and exposes the unnaturalness of copyright and its creativity-stifling claims to 'protect' intellectual 'property', again mirroring the centrality of ownership and property in Eurocentric thought. These debates in which Lessig, Graham, Gunkel and others vigorously meander, obscure modalities beyond Eurocentric thought. They calcify remix discourse to remain in the realm of newness and Western thought. Margie Borschke is clear in *This is Not a Remix*, 'Remix is neither new nor digital' (2011: 24). Understood outside of dominant regimes, the act of remixing conceptually posits and executes other modes by which humans and machines, specifically sound technologies, operate in a different yet still humanizing manner. The notion of subjugated knowledge is useful as it allows us to understand the remix as a form of local and autonomous criticism engaged in non-centralized theoretical production, whose validity is 'not dependent on established regimes of thought' (Foucault 2003). As the act of remixing adds and subtracts elements of a song it decomposes and recomposes music with an ethic of selectivity that is instructive. Remixes, cover songs, bootlegs and mash-ups creatively engage in repetition, combining difference and sameness in a myriad of ways. The ethnical selectivity in recomposing their remixes gestures towards non-dominant values, such as collaboration, homage, history and politics to interrupt the commodification process and centre well-being, audiences and the fruitful holding together of sameness and difference in sound.

As a form of criticism, the remix signifies on the vast amounts of consumer and material culture, creatively deciding how best to engage various forms of difference to produce new frames of interaction. Such local forms of criticism are strategically positioned at the bottom of the hierarchical arrangement of knowledge systems, precisely because they elaborate society's contradictions, exposing the seams of society's social constructions. As the legal battles of copyright logic versus free culture advocates rage on, remixing – a sometimes contraband activity that violates private ownership and copyright – tells us something about our current arrangements of culture as commodity and its privatization, which governing codes attempt to naturalize. Remixing tells us that our present mode of being in the West can look different when the perspectives and creative energies of those whose lives are 'out of bounds', on demonic ground, theorize ways of being human that might contribute to our well-being by growing our consciousness of connection, collaboration and engaging in the creative labour necessary for another praxis of being human.

Creative collaboration in the form of remixing suggests another mode of subjective being that is based on the creative use of sonic/social difference, not in an exploitative market-driven manner, but rather in a more egalitarian spirit of collaboration. The practice of remixing, like versioning and dub, provides us with useful methods of narrative design in which the acceptance of multiplicity and its engagements with difference provides pathways for thinking beyond our current segregated systems of knowledge. In short, 'without the ability to remix we simply cannot be human because culture becomes a passive rather than participatory interaction with the external world' (Chance 2007).

When we spend time historizing the remix, filtering out the legal concerns and focusing beyond the discursive regime of Western thought, we can then recalibrate our thinking beyond the ideal of Western bourgeois 'Man' and the over investment in conspicuous consumption, markets and rapid disposability. Dub provides templates for us to decompose and rebuild existing sonic architecture, building anew sonic subjectivities that embrace the chaotic assemblages of identification and difference. As explored in Chapter 2, as Turntablists decommodify pieces of vinyl to create new sonic landscapes, remixing – in extending dub practices – decomposes the existing components of songs, rebuilding them in a manner that resonates in new ways. By utilizing techniques popularized in the producing of dub music and combining various DJ mixing techniques and strategies (like mixtapes) and leveraging the affordances of the internet, the remix combines decades of Afrosonic innovations to pull apart and rebuild many of the discourses and hallmarks of Western musical traditions and industry. Remixing undoes the dominant arrangements of power, industry and creative praxis.

As a rich epistemological metaphor and methodological practice, remixing provides important clues as to how to live in and with the multiple possibilities of our present order. Remix as an expression of an Afrosonic episteme presents other kinds of relationalities that breech our present order of knowledge. Via the remix, we are presented with access to a sonic subjectivity whose significations disrupt musical genre, linear market time, property rights and hierarchical ordering. By relying on and extended Afrological oral and musical aesthetics, like dub, remixing's radical relationalities provide a glimpse into a more-than-'Man' formulation in which a biocentric dominance is mitigated by a rethinking of the connection of our kinaesthetics, oralities and aural aesthetic realities as the starting place of a different kind of mode of being human.

Conclusion

Come Rewind/We Were the 1st Robots

It is hard to imagine that what we deem the most natural element of our lives, our human nature, is a social construct. A neatly, yet nefariously designed 'Man' whose system of value is not only external to itself, but whose earthly creation of a monetary system overdetermines what it means to be human at this neoliberal moment. In an attempt to avoid sounding overly dramatic, I acknowledge that there are several locations on Earth where 'bourgeois man' is not the dominant modality of being human, nor is it even dominant in those places where institutions are created to reinforce the colonial project. Undoubtedly, there are a profusion of Indigenous systems of knowledge from Maori to Cree, but their worldwide popularity (if even necessary or possible) is yet to come. Despite the work of Negri and Hardt's *Empire* (2000), and other scholarly works that demonstrate multiple modernities at work (see Morley, Walcott, etc.), the evolution of Western life beyond the tenets of Enlightenment thought is slow.

What is clear, nearly half a millennium later, is that African diasporic modes of humanity were dramatically interrupted and/or rearranged by transatlantic enslavement and colonialism. Essentially, enslaved Africans in the West were arguably made into a technology, one of the first forms of 'automated' capital 'equipment' dehumanized to ensure profit and accumulation. Stripped of humanity by the limited ways that Western colonialists imagined the human, enslaved Africans as technologies of capital accumulation made foreign investors rich, resulting in the likes of Barclays bank, insurance companies and many other enduring institutions. The vicious and terrorizing ways in which humanity was consistently denied for Africans under colonialism gestures at how we can think of enslaved Africans as dehumanized robots of capital accumulation (as opposed to simply just free labour). This is not meant to rid the enslaved of all agency, but rather to reframe a horrible truth into a tool of analytical inquiry. Such an intellectual exercise is only useful to bring about a critique of modern discourses of bourgeois Man, as Wynter has brilliantly done. These forced robots/enslaved Africans lived a remixed human existence transforming from technologies of capital accumulation during the day to humans at night – imbued the stories, drumming, dancing and song of a creative ethos (Hutton 2007).

The often beautifully creative transcendence of a forced dehumanized robotic existence for enslaved Africans has played itself out in myriad ways, where, other excesses of modernity – intentionally obsolescent turntables and oil drums, for instance – are used to create other(ed) sonic subjectivities that proposes a relational mode of being human. This cultural/biological hybridization, buried within the counter-world and counter-narratives within Black popular culture, has consistently counteracted the overrepresentation of Man, allowing humanity to flourish, however fleeting and impermanent. On plantations, petit marronage, work stoppages and dramatic theatrical performances were moments where the human interrupted these forced robotic modes. Utterances of humanity broke the construction of these carefully crafted dehumanized technologies of capital accumulation. These utterances, found today in the sound system's DeeJay's ad libs, soundings and improvisations, illuminate the workings of sonic subjectivities that continue to imagine life beyond object status, beyond consumer and beyond 'Man'.

By spending significant time exploring the Afrosonic innovations, Afrosonic Life's goal – to expand the conceptual terrain of a relational modality of being human – has begun in small and humble ways. As this book moved through remix culture, dub, turntablism and other Afrosonic innovations, it became clear that it is the multiplicity and embeddedness of difference into the sonic cultures of Afrodiasporic communities that productively troubles our contemporary moment. Sonic dissonance, a heterogenous sound ideal, the mix and the remix adamantly speak truth to power, operate in other(ed) modes that starkly illuminate the inadequacy of Western epistemologies. Why this demonic ground? Why the Afrosonic explorations of niche and widely unknown musical practices? Just like the necessary and erudite work of Sylvia Wynter in her massive body of intellectual struggle or like Katherine McKittrick (2006) on Black women's geographies, we have an ethical duty to exhaust all of our resources, popular and unpopular, in an attempt to produce more equitable futures.

Explicitly, what this book has argued for is a remixed notion of the Human, a more-than-'Man' version. Taking into consideration how Enlightenment tenets such as autonomy and the 'rights of Man', and property rights structure our everyday realities in the West, the suggestion of a remixed human is not a stretch.

It is essentially calling for a more heterogeneous and expansive circulation of ideas to disrupt and reimagine Western society. By using the polyrhythmic realities of Afrodiasporic life as templates, to think through how we might balance Afrosonic subjectivities alongside the realities of Homo oeconomicus is a complex request of our modern society. What if we extrapolated the underlying premise of remix culture, a notion of creative licence with existing materials, and fashioned a system of human interactions? What of an idea of human behaviour that operates in an improvisational way to negotiate encounters of otherness, a mix that could create temporary zones of representation as DJ Spooky (2007) called them? What if ideas of how to relate to one another were based on generous encounters of the unknown as Glissant's (1997) 'donner avec' notions push us to consider? What if our modern thought systems were to operate as a DJ, mixing different ideas and moving through improvisatory poetics to negotiate our present to address immediate and local issues? These are just some of the ways in which thinking through this relational modality of being human urges us to ethically negotiate Afrosonic innovations for tools to negotiate our present.

A modernity based on creative interpretation and use of existing materials and ideas seems to me to be more current than the ideas that emanated from coffee houses in the 1600s and 1700s. Unfortunately, economic rationality reigns supreme, clearly to the detriment of the environment, future generations and all else that do not easily compute and celebrate the idea of capital accumulation. Such singular lines of thinking, this unwillingness to integrate multiple ways of knowing into modern life, have caused irreversible damage to our planet. If we can envision a parallel understanding of Western life, a polyrhythmic and remixed notion of a modernity comfortable with difference, variation and multiplicity, we can begin to balance the unilateral singular power of an economic rationalized thinking that continues to wreak havoc on our environment and the lives of the 99 per cent. A return to a sense of entanglement with nature, with other humans, with flora is what Afrosonic Life urges, performs and encourages.

In two very different ways, remix culture is a critique of the tendency of Western epistemologies to mute, eradicate or obscure social difference and the unknown – a haunting consistent action of the colonial encounter of the unknown. Remix culture unravels the normalized and uncomfortable way in which homogenous ideas and realities stunt the growth of creative ideas in very clear terms such as the innovative emergence of copyleft and the Creative Commons. But, as early proponents of remix culture (excluding Eduardo Navas and DJ Spooky) consistently erased the foundational importance of the Jamaican sound system to the remix, our traction in 'other(ed)' human modes remains unsatisfactory. Mixing the foundational ideas of remix culture alongside our contemporary moment means remixing the foundational ideas of Enlightenment thinking – listening carefully to both discourses, paying specific attention to areas in which overlap or unison might enhance human life. For example, when we think about consumerism, the unique way in which remix culture and turntablism resists manufactured obsolescence can sit comfortably alongside an understanding of consumption (and conspicuous consumption) as an activity to acquire social capital. In such a scenario, the creative consumption of DJs and music producers or of fan vids can and should be equally as valued as the overconsumptive modes of bourgeois man. The creative ways in which DJs and selectors engage existing records and samples suggests there are versions or ways in which humans can and do engage in consumption and the logic of the market as more than traditional retail consumers. There are the collectors for whom accumulation is paramount and where the acquisition of rare material items is central to how these collectors accrue value. These individuals, for instance comic book mogul Todd McFarlane or sneaker collector DJ Clark Kent, are widely accepted as accomplished and valued human beings (at least in the West); their value is enhanced by their popular media attention due to their success in their respective fields as well as their notable collections.

In contrast, the techniques of a Turntablist's transformer scratch or the wheelback of a Selector garner the studious attention of creative individuals and, thus, require us to engage the market in a different way. These creative sonic engagements do not encourage the prevailing logic of overconsumption and so media outlets pay little attention. The complex ways in which DJs, Turntablists, Dub Organizers and sound systems widen the ways in which we might imagine contemporary relationships with material culture are fruitful in terms of theoretical exploration and not as user-friendly for expanding the tentacles of late capitalism.

If we reflect back on a figure such as M.I.A. and her seamless movement between ethnicities, genres and cultures (Western, non-Western, dancehall, reggae, electro, etc.), it becomes clear that conspicuous consumption does not overdetermine her being. M.I.A.'s video for 'Bad Girls', where Saudi desert stunt racing, standing in for consumptive modes of Middle Eastern life, is juxtaposed alongside the 'other(ed)' Muslim body, is just one example of her interesting embodiment of the remix aesthetic. Across a spectrum of signs, she is fluid in her connections of differences or 'other(ed)' ways of being, yet critical of the dominant discourses of the West that racialize and criminalize the racialized brown and Muslim body. This does not mean M.I.A.'s work has not been controversial and at times charged with cultural appropriation. The ways in which limited analysis reads M.I.A. in a binary of either appropriation or celebration, obscure the ways in which her oeuvre is focused on power and diffusing the ways in which the West relegates its 'others' to valueless margins of society.

Wynter's urgent call for another mode of humanity, her call to move past 'Man', is a call for a hybrid biological and cultural mode of being. It is within this mode that we recognize 'Man's cultural creation of itself and move beyond a biological and naturalizing discourse. If we spend time with hip-hop, and see young and excessively styled racialized individuals acquiring social capital through their signified bodies at the very moment the illegible resounding of gunshots, 'bo bo bo' respond to the wheelback of the selector, this is where the hybrid human flourishes, within the counter-world of Black popular culture. Despite the biological trappings of our racialized bodies, a centralizing of the sonic as method and metaphor for another mode of being human makes Black life more liveable, actively producing and reproducing Black joy in a key inaudible to the dominant culture. The tensions are clear and brilliantly played upon by hip-hoppers whose cut 'n' mix sonic inheritance plays out in ways that make bourgeoisie clothing designers such as Tommy Hilfiger uncomfortable and innovators like Dapper Dan a brilliant remixer. It is here, a crossroads where biological lack is signified upon, that the sound system's lineage of sonic innovations reveals the seams and limits of Western 'Man'. Yet, because there exists no discursive power at this site of otherness (just templates for Black life), at this demonic ground, Western thought remains trapped in its destructively biocentric, extractive and semantically closed modality. It is my hope that eventually we will begin to listen to and live through the B-side of our contemporary moment.

Bibliography

Introduction

Barber, K. (2020), *I Could Speak Until Tomorrow: Oriki, Women & the Past in a Yoruba Town*, Edinburgh: Edinburgh University Press.

McKittrick, K. (2021), *Dear Science and Other Stories*, Durham, NC: Duke University Press.

Southern, E. (1997), *The Music of Black Americans: A History*, New York: W.W. Norton & Company.

Walcott, R. (2006), 'Salted Cod: Black Canada and Diasporic Sensibilities', in *Reading the Image: Poetics of the Black Diaspora* [exhibition catalogue], Chatham, ONT: Thames Art Gallery.

Weheliye, A.G. (2005), *Phonographies: Grooves in Sonic Afro-Modernity*, Durham: University of North Carolina Press.

Wynter, S. (1992), 'Rethinking "Aesthetics": Notes Towards a Deciphering Practice', in M. Cham (ed.), *Ex-Iles: Essays on Caribbean Cinema*, 237–279, Trenton, NJ: Africa World Press.

Chapter 1

Baker, H.A., Jr. (1984), *Blues, Ideology and Afro-American Literature: A Vernacular Theory*, Chicago: University of Chicago Press.

Barrow, S. and P. Dalton (2004), *The Rough Guide to Reggae*, 3rd edition, Toronto: Penguin Books Canada.

Bradley, L. (2000), *Bass Culture: When Reggae Was King*, Toronto: Penguin Books.

Brewster, B. and F. Broughton (2006), *Last Night a DJ Saved My Life: The History of the Disc Jockey*, New York: Open Road+ Grove/Atlantic.

Campbell, M.V. (2009), 'Remixing the Social: Pursuing Social through Music Education', in Elizabeth Gould, J. Countryman, C. Morton, and L.S. Rose (eds), *Exploring Social Justice: How Music Education Might Matter*, 359–370, Toronto: Canadian Music Educators' Association.

Césaire, A. (1972), *Discourse on Colonialism*, translated by J. Pinkham, New York: MR.

Chang, J. (2005), *Can't Stop Won't Stop: A History of the Hip-Hop Generation*, New York: St. Martin's Press.

Chude-Sokei, L. (1994), 'Post-Nationalist Geographies: Rasta, Ragga, and Reinventing Africa', *African Arts*, 27 (4): 80–96.

Cooper, C. (2004), *Sound Clash: Jamaican Dancehall Culture at Large*, New York: Palgrave Macmillan.

Diakopoulos, N., K. Luther, Y. Medynskiy, and I. Essa (2007), 'The Evolution of Authorship in a Remix Society', in *Proceedings of the Eighteenth Conference on Hypertext and Hypermedia*, September: 133–136.

Dudley, S. (2003), 'Tradition and Modernity in Trinidadian Steelband Performance', in F.R. Aparicio and C.F. Jaquez (eds), *Musical Migrations*, vol. 1, *Transnationalism and Cultural Hybridity in Latin/o America*, 147–160, New York: Palgrave Macmillan.

Fischer, S. (2015), 'Atlantic Ontologies: On Violence and Being Human', *Caribbean Rasanblaj*, 12 (1). Available online: http://archive.hemisphericinstitute.org/hemi/en/emisferica-121-caribbean-rasanblaj/fischer (accessed 5 September 2021).

Floyd, S.A., Jr. (1996), *The Power of Black Music: Interpreting Its History from Africa to the United States*, Oxford: Oxford University Press.

Gates, H.L., Jr. (1988), *The Signifying Monkey: A Theory of African American Literary Criticism*, Oxford: Oxford University Press.

Gilroy, P. (1991), 'Sounds Authentic: Black Music, Ethnicity, and the Challenge of a "Changing Same"', *Black Music Research Journal*, 11(2): 111–136.

Handler, J.S. (1982), 'Slave Revolts and Conspiracies in Seventeenth-Century Barbados', *Nieuwe West-Indische Gids/New West Indian Guide*, 56 (1/2): 5–42.

Henriques, J. (2007), 'Situating Sound: The Space and Time of the Dancehall Session', in *Sonic Interventions. Thamyris: Intersecting: Place, Sex and Race*, 287–310, New York: Rodopi.

Henriques, J. (2011), *Sonic Bodies: Reggae Sound Systems, Performance Techniques, and Ways of Knowing*, New York: Bloomsbury Publishing USA.

Howard, D.O. (2016), *The Creative Echo Chamber: Contemporary Music Production in Kingston, Jamaica*, Kingston: Ian Randle Publishers.

Hutton, C. (2007), 'The Creative Ethos of the African Diaspora: Performance Aesthetics and the Fight for Freedom and Identity', *Caribbean Quarterly*, 53 (1–2) (March–June): 127–149.

Kamugisha, A. (2016), '"That Area of Experience That We Term the New World": Introducing Sylvia Wynter's "Black Metamorphosis"', *Small Axe: A Caribbean Journal of Criticism*, 20 (1): 37–46.

Louis Chude-Sokei, L. (1994). Post-Nationalist Geographies: Rasta, Ragga, and Reinventing Africa, African Arts 27 no.4: 80–96.

Lowe, L. and K. Manjapra (2019), 'Comparative Global Humanities after Man: Alternatives to the Coloniality of Knowledge', *Theory, Culture & Society*, 36 (5): 23–48.

McKittrick, K. (2006), *Demonic Grounds: Black Women and the Cartographies of Struggle*, Minnesota: University of Minnesota Press.

McKittrick, K. (2015), 'Axis, Bold as Love: On Sylvia Wynter, Jimi Hendrix, and the Promise of Science', in *Sylvia Wynter*, 142–163, Durham, NC: Duke University Press.

McKittrick, Katherine. "Diachronic loops/deadweight tonnage/bad made measure." *cultural geographies* 23, no. 1 (2016): 3–18.

Moten, F. (2003), *In the Break: The Aesthetics of the Black Radical Tradition*, Minnesota: University of Minnesota Press.

Scott, D. (2000), 'The Re-enchantment of Humanism: An Interview with Sylvia Wynter', *Small Axe*, (8) (September): 119–207.

Snead, J.A. (1981), 'On Repetition in Black Culture', *Black American Literature Forum*, 15 (4): 146–154.

Stanley-Niaah, S. (2009), 'Negotiating a Common Transnational Space: Mapping Performance in Jamaican Dancehall and South African Kwaito', *Cultural Studies*, 23 (5–6): 756–774.

Stolzoff, N.C. (2002), *Wake the Town and Tell the People: Dancehall Culture in Jamaica*, Durham, NC: Duke University Press.

'The Third Place, Mar. 6, 1981' (1981), Cornell University Library. Available online: https://digital.library.cornell.edu/catalog/ss:1334150 (accessed 5 September 2021).

Veal, M.E. (2007), *Dub: Soundscapes & Shattered Songs in Jamaican Reggae*, Middletown, CT: Wesleyan University Press.

Walcott, R. (2006), 'Salted Cod: Black Canada and Diasporic Sensibilities', in *Reading the Image: Poetics of the Black Diaspora* [exhibition catalogue], Chatham, ONT: Thames Art Gallery.

Weheliye, A.G. (2005), *Phonographies: Grooves in Sonic Afro-Modernity*, Durham: University of North Carolina Press.

Wilson, O. (1992), 'The Heterogeneous Sound Ideal in African-American Music', *New Perspectives on Music: Essays in Honor of Eileen Southern*: 327–338.

Woods, C. (2007), '"Sittin' on Top of the World": The Challenges of Blues and Hip Hop Geography', in K. McKittick and C. Woods (eds), *Black Geographies and the Politics of Place*, 46–81, Toronto: Between the Lines.

Wynter, S. (1970), 'Jonkonnu in Jamaica: Towards the Interpretation of Folk Dance as a Cultural Process', *Jamaica Journal*, 4 (2) (June): 34–48.

Wynter, S. (1971), 'Novel and History, Plot and Plantation', *Savacou*, (5): 95–102.

Wynter, S. (1977), 'We Know Where We Are From: The Politics of Black Culture from Myal to Marley', Houston Conference, November 1977, in CLR James Collection, Africana Studies Department, Brown University.

Wynter, S. (1987), 'On Disenchanting Discourse: "Minority" Literary Criticism and Beyond', *Cultural Critique*, 7: 207–244.

Wynter, S. (1992), 'Rethinking "Aesthetics": Notes Towards a Deciphering Practice', in M. Cham (ed.), *Ex-Iles: Essays on Caribbean Cinema*, 237–279, Trenton, NJ: Africa World Press.

Wynter, S. (2003), 'Unsettling the Coloniality of Being/Power/Truth/Freedom: Towards the Human, After Man, It's Overrepresentation – An Argument', *Centennial Review*, 3 (3): 257–337.

Wynter, S. (2006), 'Proud Flesh Inter/Views: Sylvia Wynter', *Proud Flesh: New African Journal of Culture, Politics & Consciousness*, 4: 1–35.

Wynter, S. (n.d.), 'Black Metamorphosis: New Natives in a New World', unpublished manuscript.

Chapter 2

Barrow, S. and P. Dalton (2004), *The Rough Guide to Reggae*, 3rd edition, Toronto: Penguin Books Canada.

Benedictus, T. and P. Frederiske (2002), *How to DJ: The Insider's Guide to Success on the Decks*, London: Point Blank.

Bradley, L. (2000), *Bass Culture: When Reggae Was King*, Toronto: Penguin Books.

Cooper, C. (2004), *Sound Clash: Jamaican Dancehall Culture at Large*, New York: Palgrave Macmillan.

Dudley, S. (2003), 'Tradition and Modernity in Trinidadian Steelband Performance', in F.R. Aparicio and C.F. Jaquez (eds), *Musical Migrations*, vol. 1, *Transnationalism and Cultural Hybridity in Latin/o America*, 147–160, New York: Palgrave Macmillan.

Edmonds, E.B. (1998), 'Dread "I" In-A-Babylon', in N. Murrell and D. Spencer (eds), *Chanting Down Babylon: The Rastafari Reader*, ch. 1, Philadelphia: Temple University Press.

Eshun, K. (1998), *More Brilliant than the Sun: Adventures in Sonic Fiction*, London: Quarter Books.

Gilroy, P. (1987), *There Ain't No Black in the Union Jack: The Cultural Politics of Race and Nation*, 2nd edition, Chicago: University of Chicago Press.

Gilroy, P. (1991), 'Sounds Authentic: Black Music, Ethnicity, and the Challenge of a "Changing Same"', *Black Music Research Journal*, 11 (2): 111–136.

Gilroy, P. (1993), *Black Atlantic: Modernity and Double Consciousness*, London: Verso.

Hall, S. and P. du Gay, eds (1996), *Questions of Cultural Identity*, London: Sage.

Hebdige, D. (1987), *Cut 'N' Mix: Culture, Identity and Caribbean Musics*, New York: Routledge.

Hepner, R.L. (1998), 'Chanting Down Babylon in the Belly of the Beast: The Rastafarian Movement in the Metropolitan United states', *Chanting Down Babylon: The Rastafari Reader*, 199: 216.

Hisama, E.M. (2014), 'DJ Kuttin Kandi: Performing Feminism', *American Music Review*, 43 (2). Available online: http://www.brooklyn.cuny.edu/web/academics/centers/hitchcock/publications/amr/v43-2/hisama.php (accessed 15 August 2021).

Katz, M. (2010), *Capturing Sound: How Technology Has Changed Music*, Berkeley: University of California Press.

Katz, M. (2012), *Groove Music: The Art and Culture of the Hip-Hop DJ*, Oxford: Oxford University Press on Demand.

Koenigsberg, A. (1969), *Edison Cylinder Records, 1889–1912. With an Illustrated History of the Photograph*, New York: Stellar Productions.

Lorde, A. (1984), 'The Master's Tools Will Never Dismantle the Master's House', in *Sister Outsider: Essays and Speeches*, Berkeley, CA: Crossing Press.

McFarlane, A.A. (1998), 'The Epistemological Significance of "I-an-I" as a Response to Quashie and Anancyism in Jamaican Culture', in N. Murrell and W. Spencer (eds), *Chanting Down Babylon: The Rastafari Reader*, ch. 6, Philadelphia: Temple University Press.

Mudede, C. (2004), 'The Turntable', in Arthur and Marilouise Kroker (eds), *Life in the Wires*, 70–78, Victoria: CTheory Books.

Neal, M. (1999), *What the Music Said: Black Popular Music and Black Public Culture*, New York: Routledge.

Pollard, V. (2000), *Dread Talk: The Language of Rastafari*, revised edition, London: McGill-Queen's University Press.

Schloss, J.G. (2004), *Making Beats: The Art of Sample-Based Hip-Hop*, Middletown, CT: Wesleyan University Press.

Smith, S. (2016), *Hip-Hop Turntablism, Creativity and Collaboration*, Abingdon, UK: Routledge.

Toop, D. (2000), *Rap Attack #3: African Rap to Global Hip Hop*, London: Serpent's Tail.

van Koningsbruggen, P.H. (1997), *Trinidad Carnival: A Quest for National Identity*, London: Caribbean.

Van Veen, T.C. (2002), 'Vinyauralism: The Art of the Craft of Turntablism', The DJ School, Disorder, March/April. Available online: https://www.scribd.com/document/55035776/Vinyauralism-The-Art-and-the-Craft-of-Turntablism-The-DJ-School (accessed 28 January 2021).

Webber, S. (2003), *The Art of the DJ Turntables Technique*, Boston: Berklee Press.

Wilson, O. (1992), 'The Heterogeneous Sound Ideal in African-American Music', *New Perspectives on Music: Essays in Honor of Eileen Southern* (1992): 327–338.

Woods, C. (2007), '"Sittin' on Top of the World": The Challenges of Blues and Hip Hop Geography', in K. McKittick and C. Woods (eds), *Black Geographies and the Politics of Place*, 46–81, Toronto: Between the Lines.

Wynter, S. (1977), 'We Know Where We Are From: The Politics of Black Culture from Myal to Marley', Houston Conference, November 1977, in CLR James Collection, Africana Studies Department, Brown University.

Wynter, S. (2003), 'Unsettling the Coloniality of Being/Power/Truth/Freedom: Towards the Human, after Man, Its Overrepresentation – An Argument', *CR: The New Centennial Review*, 3 (3): 257–337.

Wynter, S. and K. McKittrick (2015), 'Unparalleled Catastrophe for Our Species? Or, to Give Humanness a Different Future: Conversations', in *Sylvia Wynter*, 9–89, Durham, NC: Duke University Press.

Chapter 3

Allsopp, R. and J. Allsopp, eds (2003), *Dictionary of Caribbean English Usage*, Kingston, Jamaica: University of West Indies Press.

Andrew-Gee, E. (2016), 'Sound of the 6ix: How Drake Inspired Toronto to Mint Its Own Music', *Globe and Mail*, 29 July 2016. Available online: https://www.theglobeandmail.com/news/toronto/sound-of-the-6ix-how-drake-inspired-toronto-to-mint-its-own-music/article31207071/ (accessed 11 May 2021).

Awready (2012), 'Already!: Houston Hip Hop Conference'. Available online: https://sites.lib.uh.edu/hiphop/ (accessed 18 August 2021).

Ball, J. (2010), 'Mixtape Inc. and the Definitive Incorporation of Dissent Culture', *Words. Beats. Life. The Global Journal of Hip-Hop Culture*, 3 (2): 14, 70.

Brown, J.N. (2009), *Dropping Anchor, Setting Sail*, Princeton, NJ: Princeton University Press.

Campbell, M.V. (2012), 'The Gwannings', *Jamaica in the Canadian Experience: A Multiculturalizing Presence*: 120–132.

Campbell, M.V. (2020), 'Doing the Knowledge: Digitally Archiving Hip-Hop in Canada', in C. Marsh and M.V. Campbell (eds), *We Still Here: Hip Hop North of the 49th Parallel*, 17–31, Montreal: McGill-Queen's University Press.

Clarke, G.E. (1997), 'White Like Canada', *Transitions* (73): 98–109.

Elder, S. (2016), 'Where Did Drake's "Jamaican" Accent Come From?', *Buzzfeed News*, 28 July 2016. Available online: https://www.buzzfeednews.com/article/sajaee/some-ting-borrowed (accessed 5 September 2021).

Forman, M. (2002), *The 'Hood Comes First: Race, Space, and Place in Rap and Hip-Hop*, Middleton, CT: Wesleyan University Press.

Forrester, C. (2007). 'Ethical Issues of Negotiation: An Exploratory Study of Code-Switching, Deception, and Negotiation Tactics in the Jamaican Context', in N. Cowell, A. Campbell, G. Chen and S. Moore (eds), *Ethical Perspectives for Caribbean Business*, Kingston, Jamaica: Arawak Publications.

Glissant, É. (1997), *Poetics of Relation*, translated by B. Wing, Ann Arbor: University of Michigan Press.

Gosa, Travis L. "The fifth element: Knowledge." *The Cambridge companion to hip-hop* (2015): 56–70.

Henriques, J. (2011), *Sonic Bodies: Reggae Sound Systems, Performance Techniques, and Ways of Knowing*, New York: Bloomsbury Publishing USA.

James, C.E. (2001), 'The Distorted Images of African Canadians: Impact, Implications and Responses', in C. Green (ed.), *Globalization and Survival in the Black Diaspora: The New Urban Challenge*, 307–328, New York: State University.

Lipscombe, J. (2016), 'This Is a 6 God Dream', *Exclaim!*, 16 March 2016. Available online: https://exclaim.ca/music/article/drake-this_is_a_6_god_dream (accessed 5 September 2021).

Love, Bettina L. "Knowledge reigns supreme: The fifth element, hip-hop critical pedagogy & community." In # *HipHopEd: The compilation on hip-hop education*, pp. 38–43. Brill Sense, 2018.

Lowers, E. (2016), 'Drake: King of the North', *Exclaim!*, 29 March 2016. Available online: https://exclaim.ca/music/article/drake-king_in_the_north (accessed 5 September 2021).

Madden, S. (2020), 'The Raid that Changed Rap', *NPR*, 29 October 2020. Available online: https://www.npr.org/2020/10/29/928625419/dj-drama-mixtape-raid-that-changed-rap (accessed 18 August 2021).

Manuel, P. and W. Marshall (2006), 'The Riddim Method: Aesthetics, Practice, and Ownership in Jamaican Dancehall', *Popular Music*, 25 (3): 447–470.

MarveL (1998), [vinyl] 'Internal Affairs', Toronto: Kneedeep Records.

McConnell, J. (2015) 'We the 6: Why the Name Drake Gave Us Is Here to Stay', *Globe and Mail*, 10 July 2015. Available online: https://www.theglobeandmail.com/news/toronto/we-the-6-why-the-name-drake-gave-us-is-here-to-stay/article25421112 (accessed 10 May 2021).

McKinnon, M. (2005), 'Tigress Beat: The New World Music of M.I.A', cbc.ca. Available online: http://www.cbc.ca/arts/music/mia.html (accessed 1 August 2009).

McKittrick, K. (2006), *Demonic Grounds: Black Women and the Cartographies of Struggle*, Minnesota: University of Minnesota Press.

Mufwene, S.S. (2001), *The Ecology of Language Evolution*, Cambridge: Cambridge University Press.

Phillip, M.N. (1998), 'Black W/Holes', *Fuse*, 21 (4): 27–36.

Reid, S., S. Calloway, R. Dukes, D. Byrne, H. Parry, and C. Waller (2003), 'Mixtapes: The Other Music Industry', *MTV News* 10.

RTAShowcase (2017), '"I Was There" – The Evolution of Hip Hop Radio in Canada – Part 2', YouTube, 16 May 2017. Available online: https://youtu.be/mZkXk27Wk2w (accessed 18 August 2021).

Rutherford, J. (1990), *Identity: Community, Culture, Difference*, London: Lawrence & Wishart.

Shonberger, N. (2010), 'From Party Tapes to MP3: A Cultural History of the Mixtape', *Words. Beats. Life: A Global Journal of Hip Hop Culture*, 3 (2): 8–13.

Soul Controllers (2003), [CD] *Reggae Meets Hip Hop 8*.

Wang, O. (2003), 'Tales of the Tape', *Village Voice*, 22 July 2003. Available online: https://www.villagevoice.com/2003/07/22/tales-of-the-tape/ (accessed 18 August 2021).

Wong, C. (1999), 'Toronto Stores Raided for Mixtapes', *Rolling Stone Magazine*, 7 October 1999. Available online: https://www.rollingstone.com/music/music-news/toronto-stores-raided-for-mixtapes-76641/ (accessed 28 January 2021).

Wynter, S. (n.d.), 'Black Metamorphosis: New Natives in a New World', unpublished manuscript.

Chapter 4

Baker, H.A., Jr. (1993), *Black Studies, Rap, and the Academy*, Chicago: University of Chicago Press.

Baron, Z. (2009), 'The Sri Lankan Government's War with M.I.A.', *Village Voice*, 7 April 2009. Available online: https://www.villagevoice.com/2009/04/07/the-sri-lankan-governments-war-with-m-i-a-continues/ (assessed 28 January 2020).

Barrow, S. and P. Dalton (2004), *The Rough Guide to Reggae*, 3rd edition, Toronto: Penguin Books Canada.

Boisvert, A.M. (2003), 'On Bricolage', *Horizon Zero*.

Borschke, M. (2011), 'Rethinking the Rhetoric of Remix', *Media International Australia*, 141 (1): 17–25.

Bradley, L. (2000), *Bass Culture: When Reggae Was King*, Toronto: Penguin.

Brewster, B. and F. Broughton (2014), *Last Night a DJ Saved My Life: The History of the Disc Jockey*, New York: Open Road+ Grove/Atlantic.

Broughton, F. and B. Brewster (2006), *Last Night a DJ Saved My Life: The History of the Disc Jockey*, New Centenary Edition, London: Headline.

Burton, R.D.E. (1995), 'The Idea of Difference in Contemporary French West Indian Thought: Negritude, Antillanite, Creolite', in R.D.E. Burton and F. Reno (eds), *French and West Indian: Martinique, Guadeloupe and French Guiana Today*, 137–166, London: Macmillan.

Chamberlain, J. (2010), 'So Special, So Special, So Special: The Evolution of the Jamaican Dubplate', *Jamaica Journal*, 33 (14 December 2010).

Chance, T. (2007), 'Remix Culture', *Free Software Magazine*, 15 August 2007. Available online: http://freesoftwaremagazine.com/articles/focus-music_and_remixing/ (accessed 22 December 2020).

Collins, H. (2005), 'Her Sound is the Future', *Vibe Magazine*, June 2005: 90. Available online: https://books.google.ca/books?id=-iYEAAAAMBAJ&pg=PA90&lpg=PA90&dq=Her+Sound+is+the+Future+MIA&source=bl&ots=nQSOWNS5q5&sig=ACfU3U2gcIzJaMEvopNUXZeInDFZTrmr1A&hl=en&sa=X&ved=2ahUKEwjzhKXCnMfuAhURT98KHaHAAykQ6AEwE3oECA8QAg#v=onepage&q=Her%20Sound%20is%20the%20Future%20MIA&f=false (accessed 28 January 2021).

Davis, E. (2006), 'Remixing the Matrix: An Interview with Paul D. Miller, aka DJ Spooky'.

Davis, E. (2008), '"Roots and Wires" Remix: Polyrhythmic Tricks and the Black Electronic', in P.D. Miller AKA DJ Spooky That Subliminal Kid (ed.), *Sound Unbound*, 53–72, Cambridge, MA: MIT Press.

Douglass, F. (1993), *The Life and Times of Frederick Douglass: His Early Life as a Slave, his Escape from Bondage and his Complete History*, New York Gramercy Books.

Empire, K. (2005), 'Flash Forward', *The Observer*, 20 March 2005.

Eshun, K. (1998), *More Brilliant than the Sun: Adventures in Sonic Fiction*, London: Quarter Books.

Foucault, M. (2003), '7 January 1976', in M. Bertani and A. Fontana (eds), *Society Must be Defended: Lectures at the College De France, 1975–1976*, 1–22, New York: Picador.

Gibbo Presents (2016), 'Gunz N Rozez Ft Tasha Rozez Dubplate Story Video Mix', YouTube, 9 February 2016. Available online: https://youtu.be/D9-KLycNb_k (accessed 18 August 2021).

Gilroy, P. (1987), *There Ain't No Black in the Union Jack: The Cultural Politics of Race and Nation*, 2nd edition, Chicago: University of Chicago Press.

Glissant, É. ([1997] 2005), *Poetics of Relation*, translated by B. Wing, Ann Arbor: University of Michigan Press.

Heathcott, J. (2003), 'Urban Spaces and Working-Class Expressions across the Black Atlantic: Tracing the Routes of Ska', *Radical History Review*, (87): 183–206.

Hebdige, D. (1987), *Cut 'N' Mix: Culture, Identity and Caribbean Musics*, New York: Routledge.

Henriques, J. (2011), *Sonic Bodies: Reggae Sound Systems, Performance Techniques, and Ways of Knowing*, New York: Bloomsbury Publishing USA.

Howard, D.O. (2016), *The Creative Echo Chamber: Contemporary Music Production in Kingston, Jamaica*, Kingston: Ian Randle Publishers.

Jennings, T. (2006), 'At the Crossroads', *Variant*, 25 (February): 23.

Lai, A. (2004), 'Remix and Feedback: A Roundtable Discussion', *Western Front Society*, 9 January 2004. Available online: https://front.bc.ca/events/i-am-the-remix/ (accessed 10 January 2021).

Lawrence, T. (2011), 'Disco Madness: Walter Gibbons and the Legacy of Turntablism and Remixology', *Journal of Popular Music Studies*, 20 (3): 276–329.

Lessig, L. (2002), 'Who Owns Culture?', unpublished manuscript.

Lessig, L. (2004), 'Free(ing) Culture for Remix', *Utah Law Review*: 961–976.

Lessig, L. (2007), 'Who Owns It?', unpublished manuscript.

Lewis, GE. (1996), 'Improvised Music after 1950: Afrological and Eurological Perspectives', *Black Music Research Journal*, 16 (1): 91–122.

Maira, S. (2000), 'Henna and Hip Hop: The Politics of Cultural Production and the Work of Cultural Studies', *Journal of Asian American Studies*, 3 (3): 329–369.

Manovich, L. (2007), 'What Comes after Remix', *ManovichNet*. Available online: http://manovich.net/index.php/projects/what-comes-after-remix (accessed 5 September 2021).

Maysles, P. (2002), 'Dubbing the Nation', *Small Axe*, 11: 91–111.

McKinnon, M. (2005), 'Tigress Beat: The New World Music of M.I.A.', *CBC.ca*.

McKittrick, K. (2015), 'Axis, Bold as Love: On Sylvia Wynter, Jimi Hendrix, and the Promise of Science', in *Sylvia Wynter*, 142–163, Durham. NC: Duke University Press.

McRobbie, A. (1999), *In the Culture Society: Art, Fashion and Popular Music*, New York: Routledge.
M.I.A. (2005), [CD] 'Sunshowers', *Arular*, XL, Interscope.
Miller, P.D. (2004), *Rhythm Science*, Cambridge, MA: MIT Press.
Miller, P.D. (2006), 'Heel Up, Wheel Up, Come Back, Rewind: Trojan Records'. Available online: http://djspooky.com/articles/trojan_records.html (accessed 19 June 2006).
Navas, E. (2012), *Remix Theory: The Aesthetics of Sampling*, Vienna: Springer.
Ong, W.J. (1982), *Orality and Literacy*, New York: Routledge.
Rana, S.A. and M.V. Campbell (2020), 'Reppin' Right: K'Naan as Diasporic Disruption in North American Hip-Hop', in C. Marsh and M.V. Campbell (eds), *We Still Here: Hip Hop North of the 49th Parallel*, ch. 10, Montreal: McGill-Queen's University Press.
Reynolds, G. (2009), 'A Stroke of Genius or Copyright Infringement: Mashups and Copyright in Canada', *SCRIPTed*, 6: 639.
Rojas, P. (2002), 'Bootleg Culture'. Available online: https://www.salon.com/2002/08/01/bootlegs/ (accessed 28 January 2021).
Schütze, B. (2003), 'Samples from the Heap: Notes on Recycling the Detritus of a Remixed Culture', *Horizon Zero*, 8 January 2003.
Spooky, DJ (2007), *Ghost World: A Story in Sound*. Available online: https://www.mixcloud.com/cps/dj-spooky-ghost-world-a-story-in-sound-/ (accessed 10 January 2021).
Spooky, DJ (n.d.), "DJ Spooky's Rebirth of a Nation". Available online: http://djspooky.com/rebirth-of-a-nation/ (accessed 18 August 2021).
Stolzoff, N. (2000), *Wake the Town and Tell the People: Dancehall Culture in Jamaica*, Durham, NC: Duke University Press.
Stolzoff, N.C. (2002), *Wake the Town and Tell the People: Dancehall Culture in Jamaica*, Durham, NC: Duke University Press.
Sullivan, P. (2013), *Remixology: Tracing the Dub Diaspora*, London: Reaktion Books.
Veal, M.E. (2007), *Dub: Soundscapes & Shattered Songs in Jamaican Reggae*, Middletown, CT: Wesleyan University Press.
Weheliye, A.G. (2005), *Phonographies: Grooves in Sonic Afro-Modernity*, Durham: University of North Carolina Press.
Weheliye, A.G. (2017), *Rhythms of Relation: Black Popular Music and Mobile Technologies*.
Woods, C. (2007), '"Sittin' on Top of the World": The Challenges of Blues and Hip Hop Geography', in K. McKittrick and C. Woods (eds), *Black Geographies and the Politics of Place*, 46–81, Toronto: Between the Lines.
Wynter, S. (1977), 'We Know Where We Are from: The Politics of Black Culture from Myal to Marley', Houston Conference, November 1977, in CLR James Collection, Africana Studies Department, Brown University.
Wynter, S. (1992), 'Rethinking "Aesthetics": Notes Towards a Deciphering Practice', in M. Cham (ed.), *Ex-Iles: Essays on Caribbean Cinema*, 237–279, Trenton, NJ: Africa World Press.

Conclusion

Glissant, É. (1997), *Poetics of Relation*, translated by B. Wing, Ann Arbor: University of Michigan Press.

Hutton, C. (2007), 'The Creative Ethos of the African Diaspora: Performance Aesthetics and the Fight for Freedom and Identity', *Caribbean Quarterly*, 53 (1–2) (March–June): 127–149.

McKittrick, K. (2006), *Demonic Grounds: Black Women and the Cartographies of Struggle*, Minnesota: University of Minnesota Press.

Negri, A. and M. Hardt (2000), *Empire*, Cambridge, MA: Harvard University Press.

Spooky, DJ (2007), *Ghost World: A Story in Sound*. Available online: https://www.mixcloud.com/cps/dj-spooky-ghost-world-a-story-in-sound-/ (accessed 10 January 2021).

Index

A-sides 2–3, 86
A-Trak 47
African diaspora 3–8, 15, 46, 60, 106, 121
   aesthetics 59
   creolization and indigenization 19, 60
   heterogeneity 99
   humanization 19
   Jamaica 9, 14, 17
   orality 16, 17, 18, 19, 25, 28, 30, 36, 39, 45, 49, 59, 61, 64, 65, 102, 118
   Trinidad 9, 17, 59, 60
Afrika Bambaataa 26n
Afrofuturism 107
Afrosonic innovation 5–9, 11, 14, 15–17, 21, 36, 120
   aesthetic practices 37
   breakbeat 38
   decomposing
   Man's Other 22, 23
   remix *see* remix
   repurposing 20, 41, 60
   self-fashioning 24
   scratching
   subversion 18–19, 31, 60, 71
   turntablism *see* turntablism
Alcapone, Dennis 69
audience participation 8, 27, 28, 40, 96
autonomy 15, 40, 61, 62, 65, 120

B-sides 2–3, 14–17, 26–7, 68, 86, 89–90, 97
DJ Babu 45, 47
Baby Blue Sound Crew 74, 75n
Badman 83
Baker, Houston A. 25, 96n
Ball, Jared 73n, 74, 75
Barber, K. 3n
Barthes, Roland 103
Bass Odyssey 32, 34–5
Beat Junkies 45
Beck 48

Beenie Man 76
Beyoncé 75
Big Daddy Kane 78
biocentricity 16, 18, 20–6, 40, 89, 118
Black Cat 84, 85
Black consciousness 99
Black creative praxis 10
Black geographies 89
Black joy 4, 16, 19, 35, 36, 64
Black liberation 5, 7
Black living 16, 25, 40, 64
Black pain 4–5
Black popular culture 120
Black Power 71n
Black pride 71n
Black well-being 64–6
Blige, Mary J. 73
Blondie 48
blues 25
body tricks 54, 60, 61
BombSquad 109
Born, Georgina 93
Borschke, Margie 93, 117
bourgeois man 16, 18, 105, 106
Boyz II Men 32
break boys 14
breakbeat 38
DJ Breakout 72
Brown, James 3, 38
DJ Brucie B 72
Busta Rhymes 75

Cage, John 46–7
call and response 27, 28, 29, 33, 35, 37, 38, 47, 63, 69
Campbell, Clive 14
Canada 47, 72
   see also Toronto
capital accumulation 16, 19, 21, 55, 119, 120
capitalism 70, 83, 104

capoeira 4
Cartesian thought 21, 22, 27, 37, 38
DJ Cash Money 51, 53–4, 56, 57, 60
Césaire, A.
Chase, Tara 85
Cheese 51–3, 56, 60–1
Choclair
Christianity 17
   Man1 18
   spirituals 5, 6, 38
Chuck D 108, 109
DJ Clark Kent 26n
classical/art music 14, 15, 97
Clinton, George 84
DJ Clue 73, 74
Coca Cola 100
cognition autonomy 62, 65
DJ Coke La Rock 26n
Cole, Leroy 32
collaboration 117
colonialism 10, 16, 17, 18, 19, 20, 27, 36–7, 39, 49, 56, 58, 62, 64, 65, 69, 70n, 104, 119
commodification 16, 21n, 22, 50, 53, 55, 56
communal experience 37
competitions 47
copyright 47, 70, 98, 103, 106–10, 117
Count Machuki 29, 109
Covey, Edward 106
crab scratch 44n
creating in the 'red' 6, 7
Creative Commons 98
creativity 31
creolization 19
crossfader 1, 32, 43
cultural dominance 15
Cuttin's Cole 32

Daddy-O Daylie 45
dance 19
dance halls 13–14, 19, 20, 27, 28, 32, 43, 63
dancehall (music)
Davis, Erik 91, 93
decentring 28, 32, 36, 81
decipherment 17–20
decommodification 53, 57–61
DeeJays 26, 29

   wheelbacks 11, 31–8
   see also DJs; Selectors
Def Jam records 109
demonic ground 7, 17, 18, 19, 117, 120, 123
DJ Diplo 97, 112, 113
disc jockeys 20n, 26, 45, 54
   see also DeeJays; DJs; Selectors
discourse of normality 15
Diwali riddim 68
DJs 1–3, 8, 9, 11, 13, 20–1
   battles 77
   creativity 31
   decipherment 17–20
   emotional sensitivity 29–30
   mixing 70
   subversion 18–19
   wheelbacks 11, 31–8
   see also DeeJays; disc jockeys; Selectors
dominant cultural logic 15
DJ Dopey 43, 44, 45, 49, 51, 56
Douglas, Frederick 101n, 106
Dr. Dre 43
Dr Hepcat 45
Drake 88
DJ Drama 74, 75n
'dread talk' 63, 65, 66
drum and bass 1
drumming 17
   steel drums 20, 59, 60, 91
Du Champ, Marcel 97
dub 4, 40, 63, 68
   remix and 91, 93, 94–7, 98, 102–6, 115–18
Dub Organizers 95–6
Dudley, Shannon. 17n
Duke Vin 32

e-waste 50
Easy 70
echo 113
Edison, Thomas 46
emcees 26n, 45
emancipation 65
empowerment 37
Engineers 26
Enlightenment 10, 21, 61, 62, 68, 119, 120, 122

enslavement 24, 39, 49, 64, 65, 105–6, 119, 120
  plantation system 17, 19
Eshun, Kodwo 60, 107
essentialism 51
Eurocentrism 2, 8, 40, 49, 56, 63, 65, 79, 102, 105, 117

Fatona, Andrea 101, 113
Faziah 88
female collaboration 48
DJ Grandmaster Flash 26n, 43, 48, 53, 72
Flavour Flav 108, 109
Flex riddim 68
Floyd, Samuel 4, 25, 66
folklore 19, 102–3
Forbes, Vincent 32
Ford-Smith, Honor 101
Fresh, Dougie 53
funk 14, 54
Furtado, Nelly 48

gangster rap 84, 85
Garvey, Marcus 62n, 83
Garveyism 62, 79
Gibbons, Walter 62n, 91
Gillis, Greg 99
Gilroy, Paul 55
Girl Talk 97, 99
Glissant, Édouard. 116, 121
griots 2
Guerrero, Vincente 101n
Guyana 80

Haile Selassie 62
Handler, Jerome S. 19n
Hardt, M. 119
Hebdige, Dick. 107
hegemonic power 15, 70
Hendrix, Jimi 35
Henriques, Julian 5, 24, 35, 71
Herc *see* Kool Herc
Herculords 26n
heteronormativity 92
hip-hop 1, 39, 44, 45, 49, 54
Hisama, Ellie 4
Hopeton, Red 32

Houston, Texas 72, 74
humanization 19
Hutton, Clinton 4, 20
hypermasculinity 33

I-Roy 69
Imperial JC 26n
improvisation 14, 24, 27, 28, 29, 38
Incredible Bongo Band 49
indigenization 19
individualism 64
innovations *see* Afrosonic innovations
instrumental versions 27
insurrection 19n, 40
interactivity 35
IRS 84–7

J Dilla 39
Jamaica 9, 14, 17
  Copyright Act 70n
  patwa 62, 80, 82, 113–14
  Uptown-Downtown divide 33
Jamaican Diaspora 9, 14, 26, 67
Jamaican soundsystem culture 5, 11, 13, 17, 26–31, 32, 67
Jaylib 6
DJ Jazzy Jeff 13, 40
Jordan Fusion shoes 100
JoyRide 68
Jwyze 76

K4ce 87
Kahlo, Frida 101n
Kamuguisha, Aaron 4
DJ Kid Capri 73
Kid Cudi 110–12
Kid Kut 75n
Killa Jewel 48
King Jammy 111
King Stitt 29
King Tubby 3, 9, 93, 95, 113, 115
K'naan 107, 110–12, 116
knowledge of self 71
Knuckles, Frankie 30, 62n, 91
Kool Herc 14, 26, 30, 38, 105
Korrey Deez 84, 85
Kuhn, Virginia 93
Kuttin' Kandi 48

L. L. Cool J 53, 57, 113
labouring Black body 16, 20, 21, 22, 27, 28, 30, 35, 60–1
Lai, Adrienne 101
Lamming, George 25
Law of Seven 1–2
Lawrence, Tim 62n
LeBrew 26n
Lee, Spike 25
Lessig, Lawrence 92, 98, 117
Levan, Larry 62n
Lewis, George 9
LGBTQ culture 92
liberal democracies 58
liberal humanism 5, 6, 15, 23, 24, 38, 64, 103, 104
liberation 5, 7, 22, 38, 59, 63, 103, 105
linguistic innovation 61–6, 79–82, 84
Long, Edward 17n
Lowe, L. 18n

M. I. A. 107, 112–15, 116
Mad House Records 70
Madonna 97
Maestro Fresh Wes 78
Man 0.0 105
Man1/Man2 18, 23, 27, 39, 58
Mandela, Nelson 99
Manjapra, K. 18n
Manley, Michael 59n
Manovich, Lev 92
Man's Other 22, 23, 28
Manuel, Peter 67, 69
market economy 6, 8, 14–15, 19, 20, 40
    capital accumulation 16, 19, 21, 55, 119, 120
    commodification 16, 21n, 22, 50, 53, 55, 56
    decommodification 53, 57–61
    extraction and waste 50
    overconsumption 50, 56
market time 36, 37
Marley, Robert Nestor 9, 92n
Maroon communities 106
Marshall, Wayne 67, 69
MarveL 80
Mason-Dixon Line 6

DJ Mastermind 74, 77
Maysles, Philip 95
McConnell, John 88n
McKittrick, Katherine 4, 5, 7, 22, 23, 105, 120
MC Lyte 78
Mee, Michie 78
Merritone Soundsystem 93
Metro Mix Offs 77
Miami 9
Mighty Crown 77
Miss Lou 61
mixtapes 16, 68, 70, 72–7
modernities 60, 91, 119
Monolith
Monroe Doctrine 60
Moore, Thurston 72
Moten, Fred 38
Motown 92
Moulton, Tom 30, 98
MSFB 98
Mufwene, Salikoko S. 81

narrative originality 102–3
Navas, Eduardo 93, 98
Negri, A. 119
Nelson, Ron 78
New York City 13, 14, 26, 46, 68, 72, 73, 74, 78
    Twelve Tribes 63
Nike 100
normality 15

Oakenfold, Paul 97
objecthood 62, 63
objectification of women 32, 33, 85
ocular-centricity 5, 8, 16, 18, 21, 28, 30, 40, 105
oil drums 20, 59, 60
Ong, Walter J. 91, 102, 103
ontological autonomy 16, 25
oppression 65, 66, 69, 105
orality 16, 17, 18, 19, 25, 28, 30, 36, 39, 45, 49, 59, 61, 64, 65, 102, 118
originality 102–3
oriki praise singers 3n
overconsumption 50, 56

Paragons 13–14
participation 8, 27, 28, 40, 96
Patra 79
patwa 62, 80, 82, 113–14
Paul, Sean 76
Pepperseed riddim 68, 70
Perry, Lee Scratch 40, 93
philip, nourbeSe 3n
phonographies 6
physicality 8, 71
    body tricks 54, 60, 61
    kinesthesia 1, 2, 5, 7, 8, 16, 25, 37, 38, 39
plantation system 17, 19
politics 99
Pollard, Velma 62
polyrhythms 28, 66, 69, 91, 92, 106
postmodernism 60
power relations 102
Prime, Jimmy 87
Prince Jammy 78, 95
Public Enemy 107, 108–10, 116

Queen 48
queer life 92
Quelbe 59

racial exclusion 105
Ramsey, Guthrie 4
Rasta culture 92
    Dread talk
Rastafari 59n, 61–5, 79, 83
RastafarI 11
rebellion 17, 106
'red' (in the) 6, 7
Redwood, Ruddy 13–14, 20
reggae 14
reggaeton 68
rehumanization 7, 27, 29, 39
Reid, Duke 13, 34, 93, 114
relationality 14, 33, 35, 53
remix 12, 17, 91–4, 116, 121–2
    contemporary engagements 97–102
    copyright 98, 103, 106–10, 117
    dub and 91, 93, 94–7, 98, 102–6, 115–18
    extended remix 98

K'naan 107, 110–12, 116
M. I. A. 107, 112–15, 116
    narrative originality 102–3
    Public Enemy 107, 108–10, 116
    reflexive remix 98
    selective remix 98
repurposing 20, 41, 60
revolution 106
rewinding 1–2, 32, 34
riddim 11, 67–71, 89–90, 95
    hip-hop and 11, 68, 72, 75, 77, 78, 83, 85, 89, 90
    mixtapes 68, 70, 72–7
    Toronto 77–87
Riel, Louis 101n
Riley, Teddy 97
Robinson, Dylan 4
Roc Raida 61
Rock, Pete 108–9, 110, 111, 112
DJ Ron G 73, 74, 77
Rose, Tricia 6
Rosez, Tasha 94n
rudeness 83
Rumble 78
Rutherford, J. 81–2

Saint Croix 59
Saint Vincent 80
Samba 59n
sampling 47
Saukrates
Scratch Band 59
scratching 13, 15, 20, 23, 31, 40, 43
DJ Screw 72
Selectors 19, 20, 21, 26, 27, 29, 30, 32, 34, 35, 37, 50, 70, 71
self-fashioning 24
self-liberation 5
Shabba Ranks 79
ska 67
DJ Kay Slay 73n
Slick Rick 53
Sneed, James 35
soca 68, 70, 71
social class 33
soft drinks 100
Somalia 110, 111, 112

sonic innovation *see* Afrosonic innovation
sonic subjectivities 6, 16, 19, 20–6, 28, 32, 37, 40, 68, 71, 89, 90, 95, 120
Soul II Soul 97
Soul Controllers 76
soul music 26
sound clash 94n
sound thinking 6
soundsystems 5, 11, 13, 17, 20, 26–31, 32, 93
spirituals 5, 6, 38
DJ Spooky 96, 97, 99, 107, 112, 121
steel drums 20, 59, 60, 91
Stone Love 32, 33, 34
subjectivities *see* sonic subjectivities
subversion 18–19, 31, 60, 71
Sugar Ray 48
Sun Rah 84

Technics 50
technologies 50
Temptations 92
Terminator X 108, 109
Theodore 46, 48
thinking sound 6
Thompson, Errol 93, 113
Timmy Tim 26n
toasting 20, 61
Toronto 9, 68, 71, 74, 75, 77–87, 89–90, 101
    6ix 87–8
Tosh, Peter 92n
transformer scratch 13
Trinidad 9, 17, 59, 60
Triple 'S' 1
Trojan sound 93
turntables 1, 2, 3, 4, 16, 20–1
turntablism 11, 40–1, 43–56
    Black well-being 65–6
    decommodifying 57–61
    historical embeddedness 61–5
Twelve Tribes 63

U-Roy 26, 69, 109
United Kingdom 9, 67
Uptown-Downtown divide 33
use value 14

Vargas, Getúlio 59n
Veal, Michael 4, 93, 94, 115
versioning 28, 91, 92
vinyl records 1–3
    obsolescence 50
Virgin Islands 59
Virgin Records 74

Wailer, Bunny 92n
Wailing Wailers 92
Walcott, Rinaldo 2n
Wall, Paul 72n
Warhol, Andy 97
Weheliye, Alexander 6, 8, 15
West, Kanye 10, 109
Western art music 14, 15, 97
Western modernity 2, 3, 10, 14–17
    Cartesian thought 21, 22, 27, 37, 38
    Man1/Man 18, 23, 27, 39
wheelbacks 11, 31–8, 50, 103–4
white supremacy 5, 30
whiteness 18
Williams, Eric 59
Wilson, Delroy 59n
Wilson, Olly 35, 53, 69
Windrush Generation 9, 67
Winstons 38
Wio-K 80
women 34, 120
    binarism 85
    female collaboration 48
    objectification 32, 33, 85
    rudeness 83
Woods, Clyde 17
Wynter, Sylvia 4, 10, 13, 14–15, 17, 18, 19, 22, 25, 38, 39, 40, 56, 58, 67, 89, 120

youth popular culture 100

www.ingramcontent.com/pod-product-compliance
Lightning Source LLC
Chambersburg PA
CBHW061843300426
44115CB00013B/2489